English Without Tears:
Mind Your P's and Q's

Peter W. Vakunta

Langaa Research & Publishing CIG
Mankon, Bamenda

Publisher:
Langaa RPCIG
Langaa Research & Publishing Common Initiative Group
P.O. Box 902 Mankon
Bamenda
North West Region
Cameroon
Langaagrp@gmail.com
www.langaa-rpcig.net

Distributed in and outside N. America by African Books Collective
orders@africanbookscollective.com
www.africanbookscollective.com

ISBN-10: 9956-552-20-8

ISBN-13: 978-9956-552-20-7

© Peter W. Vakunta 2022

All rights reserved.
No part of this book may be reproduced or transmitted in any form or by any means, mechanical or electronic, including photocopying and recording, or be stored in any information storage or retrieval system, without written permission from the publisher

Dedication

To my offspring—
Linda, Delphine, Winston, Aristide and Rodney

Acknowledgements

In a few chapters of this book, I have used excerpts culled from my articles published in newspapers in the Republics of Cameroon and South Africa in 1990s. I would like to express my profound gratitude to Editors-in-Chief of the following publications for granting me permission to reuse my material. I am referring to the *Northern Times*, *Northern Review* and *Northern Monitor* located in the city of Polokwane in the Limpopo Province in South Africa. I would be remiss if I did not express my gratitude to Mr. Patrick Mbawa, owner and editor-in-Chief of the *Cameroon Post* weekly newspaper located in the city of Yaoundé in the Republic of Cameroon. My sincere thanks also go to the *Cameroon Radio and Television Corporation (CRTV)* in Yaoundé-Cameroon, where some of the material used in this book became available to the Cameroonian audience within the framework of an English Language Program named *Better English that* I co-hosted with renowned journalist Mr. Kenneth Asobo.

I have not overlooked the opportunity offered me by the South African Broadcasting Corporation (SABC) code-named (THOBELA-FM) to use excerpts from my published articles to educate students in South Africa.

Doubtlessly, a work of this magnitude would never have seen the light of day without recourse to books published by my precursors in the field. In writing this book, I have had to consult dictionaries, grammar books, manuals and reference works in the field of second language acquisition and linguistics. To these authors alive and of blessed memory, I say thank you. My indebtedness to them in gigantic. Last but not the least, I thank to my students past and present whose heckling questions egged me onto further research into the mechanics of the English Language.

"If language is not correct, then what is said is not what is meant; if what is said is not what is meant, then what ought to be done remains undone."
Confucius in the Complete Plain Words (1979:159)

Foreword

English without Tears: Mind Your P's and Q's is a practical reference book intended for use by speakers for whom the English language is not a native tongue. Communicators who constantly lapse into grammatical errors associated with poor mastery of the mechanics of English grammar will find this book handy. There is no denying the fact that poor mastery of the rules of grammar could hamper effective communication. This is true for both native speakers as well as second language speakers of English. Communicative problems could be compounded by the multiplicity of languages spoken in multicultural/multilingual communities the world over. We are well aware of the infusion of borrowed words and expressions into the English language due to globalization and the ubiquity of information technology.

There is a myth among second language speakers of the English language that expressions that have used repeatedly is undoubtedly correct. This is an erroneous notion. We have tried to dispel this misconception by illustrating through the frequency of some of errors in the speech of second language speakers of English that frequency of usage is not synonymous with correct usage. It is our hope that this book would go a long way to alleviating these language-related problems. We believe that *English without Tears: Mind Your P's and Q's* would be a welcome addition to the large stock of books that exist on this subject matter. We are particularly desirous of making this book serve as a classroom manual for both students and teachers of English. To this end, we have included exercises at the end of each chapter, designed to assist teachers in assessing learners' understanding of issues addressed in the book.

In total, *English without Tears: Mind Your P's and Q's* comprises thirty-five chapters, each intended to serve as a point of departure for in-depth classroom discussion on specific aspects of English grammar. Each chapter starts with an explanation of key grammatical concepts and ends with evaluation exercises geared toward gauging learners' grasp of lessons taught. Answers to these exercises are located in the section labelled 'Answer Key.' An index follows the Answer Key section.

Table of Contents

Foreword vii

1. Ambiguity 1
2. Articles 5
3. Barbarisms 11
4. Capital Letters 15
5. Circumlocution 19
6. Clumsy Expressions 23
7. Collocation 31
8. Comparatives and Superlatives 35
9. Concord 39
10. Determiners 47
11. Gerunds 51
12. Homophones 55
13. Idioms 61
14. Infinitives Wrongly Used 65
15. Lexical Errors 71
16. Malapropisms 77
17. Misrelated Participles 81
18. Misspellings 87
19. Modifiers 91
20. Negation 97
21. Number 101
22. Omissions 109
23. Parts of Speech 113
24. Prepositions 117
25. Pronouns 123
26. Punctuation Marks 131
27. Quantifiers 135
28. Reported Speech 141
29. Subjective and Objective Cases 145
30. Subjunctive Mood 149
31. Synonyms 153
32. Tautology 157
33. Tenses 163
34. Verbs 173
35. Words Commonly Confused 179

36. Cameroonisms & Camerounismes 187
37. Revision Activities 199
38. Answer Key 201

Selected Bibliography 233
Index 237

Chapter 1

Ambiguity

The focus of this lesson is 'ambiguity' in English. Grammarians use this term to describe a communication situation where meaning is unclear as a result of sentences having multiple meanings. Thus, an ambiguous sentence would be one that may be interpreted in two or more ways.

Generally, ambiguity stems from the following:
(i) Misplaced phrases
(ii) Unrelated or dangling participles
(iii) Incorrectly placed adverbs

We shall use a couple of examples to drive home the point.

Example 1
- The student is looking for a small flat where she can cook herself on a hot plate. (*ambiguous*)
- The student is looking for a small flat where she can cook on a hot plate for herself. (*explicit*)

The first sentence could be interpreted to mean that the student would cook not food but herself on a hot plate.

Putting the phrase "for herself" at the end of the sentence clears the ambiguity.

Example 2
- A woman carrying her baby and her husband entered the room. (*ambiguous*)
- A woman, accompanied by her husband, entered the room carrying her baby. (*explicit*)

The second sentence is clear (unambiguous) because the dangling present participle "carrying" has been moved to the end of the sentence. The first sentence could be interpreted to mean that the woman was carrying both her baby and her husband.

Example 3
- The lady and her dog wearing a bikini darted across the road. (*ambiguous*)

- The lady wearing a bikini darted across the road with her dog. (*explicit*)

The first sentence gives the impression that the dog and not the lady was wearing a bikini. Ambiguous sentences may result in loss of meaning. Sometimes they are plainly ridiculous.

Example 4

- We are selling babies and men's clothes in this supermarket. (*ambiguous*)
- We are selling clothes for babies and men in this supermarket. (*explicit*)

Example 5

- This theatre is open to pupils only between 14HOO-16HOO. (*ambiguous*)
- This theatre is only open to pupils between 14HOO-16HOO. (*explicit*)

Sentence construction is a slippery aspect of English grammar. English speakers should pay extra attention to the positioning of modifiers and participles in order to avoid ambiguity.

EXERCISE 1

Identify the ambiguity in the sentences that follow. Rewrite each sentence avoiding the ambiguity.

a) Dogs will be brought, fleas taken off and returned to their owners for only one rand.

b) An old lady wants cleaning twice a month.

c) Firmly pierced by a fork, Peter held an oyster over the fire.

d) The umbrella was misplaced by a teenager with brass ribs.

e) The right thing to do with children who write abusive letters is to throw them into the dustbin.

f) Drinking very fast, the bottle of red wine was soon emptied.

g) These houses were constructed roughly five years back.

h) If you take your cat on a drive, don't let it hang out of the window while driving.

i) Environmental health crisis: Ad hoc committee to sit on litter.

j) Sipho and Sons: Dispensing Chemists. We dispense with expertise.

EXERCISE 2

Rewrite the following sentences so as to render them unambiguous.

a) Being in a poor condition, Sifiso was able to buy the car cheap.

b) Woman wanted to look after a baby who does not smoke.

c) Mabasa has hunted and shot himself, so he knows what he is talking about.

d) If the child would not eat the potato, mash it into a pulp.

e) When the Queen Mother had christened the ship, she disappeared into the water.

f) Mrs. Mbeki is expecting her fifth child in a couple of months.

g) My uncle attempted to kill himself by firing a pistol at his head which he kept under the pillow.

h) At the age of two her mother passed away.

i) The little girl saw a python going to fetch water.

j) Crossing the bridge a ghastly car accident could be seen.

Chapter 2

Articles

This lesson highlights some common errors stemming from the misuse of <u>articles</u>. There are two types of articles in English, namely the <u>definite article</u> (<u>the</u>) and the indefinite articles (<u>a</u> and <u>an</u>). <u>An</u> is used before words that begin with a <u>vowel</u> or mute 'h', e.g. <u>an</u> egg, <u>an</u> elephant, <u>an</u> apple, <u>an</u> orange, <u>an</u> honour, etc.

Example 1

- My granny gave me <u>an</u> advice that changed my life radically. *(wrong)*
- My granny gave me <u>some</u> advice that changed my life radically. *(correct)*   **OR**
- My granny gave me a piece of advice that changed my life radically. *(correct)*

Advice is an uncountable noun that does not require an article. However, when advice means 'formal notification' in a business context, it should be preceded by an article. For example, the personnel manager received <u>an</u> advice from the head office in Durban yesterday.

Example 2

- Miss Suleman Ayesha does not need <u>a</u> medical attention. *(wrong)*
- Miss Suleman Ayesha does not need medical attention. *(correct)*

<u>Attention</u> is a non-count noun that doesn't warrant the use of an indefinite article as seen in sentence 1 above.

Example 3

- Mr. Essack Dada found himself in insurmountable difficulties and asked for <u>a</u> help. *(wrong)*
- Mr. Essack Dada found himself in insurmountable difficulties and asked for help. *(correct)*

<u>Help</u> may be preceded by an indefinite article when it follows some part of the verb <u>be</u>. E.g. Her niece was <u>a</u> great help to her when she lost her job.

Example 4
- I would appreciate if you would come and have a lunch with me on Sunday. (wrong)
- I would appreciate if you would come and have lunch with me on Sunday. (correct)

Lunch, dinner, supper, etc. should not be preceded by an article as seen in sentence 1 above. Note, however, an article is indispensable when reference is made to a specific meal or when a choice is implied. E.g. A lunch at the Carousel Restaurant is quite expensive.

Learners of English often commit errors attributable to the omission of articles. This lesson seeks to highlight some of these mistakes.

Example 1
- Tell Mpho that if he continues to drive at that speed, he will have accident. *(wrong)*
- Tell Mpho that if he continues to drive at that speed, he will have an accident. *(correct)*

Example 2
- We didn't have chance to meet the MEC for Education yesterday. *(wrong)*
- We didn't have the chance to meet the MEC for Education yesterday. *(correct)*

Chance may function as a verb in some cases. As a verb, it is generally followed by 'to + verb.' For instance, we chanced to meet the man we were looking for (= we happened to meet the man we were looking for).

Example 3
- After drinking a whole crate of beer, Mulindwa had headache. *(wrong)*
- After drinking a whole crate of beer, Mulindwa had a headache. *(correct)*

The indefinite article a may be committed in front of toothache and stomach-ache.

Example 4
- Mochelo went home straight from the gym to take bath. *(wrong)*

- Mochelo went home straight from the gym to take a bath. *(correct)*

To have a bath is synonymous with <u>to take a bath</u>.

Example 5
- Kekana thinks he will make name for himself by impersonating. *(wrong)*
- Kekana thinks he will make a name for himself by impersonating. *(correct)*

'To make a name for oneself' means 'become well-known.' 'To impersonate a person' means 'pretend to be that person.'

Example 6
- It may come as great surprise to many people that some children are born with HIV virus. *(wrong)*
- It may come as a great surprise to many people that some children are born HIV virus. *(correct)*

Users of English often fall into the trap of misusing the definite article <u>the</u> in their daily conversation. It is noteworthy that not all nouns have to be preceded by the definite article. Speakers of English should remember that nouns may make <u>specific</u> or <u>generic</u> reference to objects. The definite article is generally used with uncountable nouns that make specific reference.

It is omitted before uncountable nouns that make <u>generic</u> reference.

Example 1
- <u>The</u> society disapproves of children who disobey their parents. *(wrong)*
- Society disapproves of children who disobey their parents. *(correct)*

The use of the definite article <u>the</u> in sentence 1 is uncalled for. However, you may use <u>the</u> if the word society were written with a capital letter, meaning a professional body. For example, the Pietersburg Debating Society.

Example 2
- Developing countries spend colossal sums of money on <u>the</u> defence. *(wrong)*
- Developing countries spend colossal sums of money on defence. *(correct)*

The use of the article <u>the</u> in sentence 1 above is unwarranted.

Example 3

- UNESCO insists that all children should go to <u>the</u> school. *(wrong)*
- UNESCO insists that all children should go to school. *(correct)*

'School' is used here as a generic (general) term. That is why the use of <u>the</u> is unnecessary.

Example 4

- Scientists have proven that <u>the</u> light travels at a speed of 180,000 miles per second. *(wrong)*
- Scientists have proven that light travels at a speed of 180,000 miles per second. *(correct)*

<u>Light</u> in this context refers to light in general, not a specific type of light. The article <u>the</u> is not needed.

Example 5

- When Wilson Sekepe left Moria, he stopped going to <u>the</u> church. *(wrong)*
- When Wilson Sekepe left Moria, he stopped going to church. *(correct)*

<u>Church</u> begins with a capital letter and is preceded by the definite article <u>the</u> when it refers to an institution. For instance, the faithfuls sometimes re-examine the doctrines of <u>the</u> Church.

However, the definite article is not needed when <u>church</u> is used as an adjective before a noun that makes a generic reference. For example, I am very interested in <u>church</u> matters.

EXERCISE 1

Underline all definite and indefinite articles in the following passage.

Now that we have moved into a new millennium, many of us stand at the crossroads. Some of us will have questions on what this new millennium holds in store for us, others about whether they will get jobs or sustain their jobs, whether the sun will shine graciously or will the world plunge into darkness.

Regardless of the time-shift we are experiencing, there is also a call from our Constitution to improve the quality of life of all citizens. Within the Bill of Rights it is clearly written that everyone has inherent dignity and the right to have their dignity respected and protected. Many South Africans have contracted the killer-disease AIDS. It is not for us to be judgemental about such people, but rather our task is to understand what healthy living is about. One could do that by conveying information, beliefs, opinions and feelings. These would show respect for self and others and the ability to advocate personal, family and community health (Prof. Kader Asmal - *South African Minister of National Education*).

EXERCISE 2

Correct the errors in the sentences that follow by inserting <u>a</u>, <u>an</u> or <u>the</u> in the blank spaces.

a) The teacher asked the pupils not to make____noise.

b) The speaker made____impression on the audience.

c) The old man didn't make____will before his death.

d) _____ hundred years ago this town was a village.

e) _____ Dutch are heavy drinkers.

f) The man makes_____fortune by selling drugs.

g) You have made_____attempt to improve on your performance.

h) Manamela drank half__glass of wine at the party.

i) _____ Catholic Church disapproves of abortion.

j) He eats four times____day.

Chapter 3

Barbarisms

In this lesson we shall discuss the concept of <u>barbarism</u> in the English language, especially the manner in which it may create unintelligibility in communication. A <u>barbarism</u> is a word formed in an unorthodox way. It conveys no more pejorative an implication other than that it is the sort of language usage that might be expected from a foreign speaker of English. Barbarism may be described as 'illiterate' expressions. A fundamental problem as far as <u>barbarisms</u> are concerned is that the foreign speaker may lack the information that would enable him/her to decide whether any particular word is or is not a barbarism. That barbarisms exist is a pity but to spend time denouncing those who are guilty of these miscreations is a waste. It will not be possible here to lay down rules for word formation, which is a complicated business, but a few examples of barbaric usages of words in English may perhaps instill caution and illustrate the point that word-making, like other manufactures, should be done by those who know how to do it (i.e. philologists).

Example 1
- After studying your order, we will send you a quotation without <u>delayance</u>. *(wrong)*
- After studying your order, we will send you a quotation without <u>delay</u>. *(correct)*

The word <u>delayance</u> in sentence 1 is a miscreation. It does not exist in English.

Example 2
- The journey to the Kruger National Park was tedious and <u>discomfortable</u>. *(wrong)*
- The Journey to the Kruger National Park was tedious and <u>uncomfortable</u>. *(correct)*

The word <u>discomfortable</u> in sentence 1 is a spurious hybrid.

Example 3
- I should like to extend my <u>gladful</u> thanks to all the volunteers. *(wrong)*

• I should like to extend my <u>thanks</u> to all the volunteers. *(correct)*

'Gladful' in sentence 1 is a misformation. Note that 'greatful' is also a miscreation.

Example 4

• All travel arrangements are subject to <u>conformation</u> by the travel agency. *(wrong)*

• All travel arrangements are subject to <u>confirmation</u> by the travel agency. *(correct)*

The word <u>conformation</u> in sentence 1 above is a barbarism.

Example 5

• Mr. Wilson Mpyana explained <u>detailly</u> the events of yesterday. *(wrong)*

• Mr. Wilson Mpyana explained <u>in detail</u> the events of yesterday. *(correct)*

The aim of this lesson is to spotlight some common illiteracies that constitute communication pitfalls to quite a few speakers of English.

Example 1

• Could you please <u>borrow</u> me your book, Molema? *(wrong)*

• Could you please <u>lend</u> me your book, Molema? *(correct)* It is important to stress that the person who <u>borrows</u> is the one who <u>takes</u>; the one who <u>lends</u> is the person who <u>gives</u>.

Example 2

• There's likely to be a cabinet <u>reshufflement</u> before the end of the year. *(wrong)*

• There's likely to be a <u>cabinet reshuffle</u> before the end of the year. *(correct)*

When a political leader changes the jobs of his/her ministers in such a way that each one of them assumes a different portfolio, we say there has been a cabinet <u>reshuffle</u>.

Example 3

• Most South Africans are clamouring for the <u>abolishment</u> of euthanasia. *(wrong)*

• Most South Africans are clamouring for the <u>abolition</u> of euthanasia. *(correct)*

The noun derived from the verb <u>abolish</u> is <u>abolition</u>.

Example 4
- The girl failed the interview because of her extreme ignorancy. *(wrong)*
- The girl failed the interview because of her extreme ignorance. *(correct)*

The noun derived from the adjective ignorant is ignorance.

Example 5
- The pronounciation of this lengthy word is very difficult. *(wrong)*
- The pronunciation of this lengthy word is very difficult. *(correct)*

The noun derived from the verb pronounce is pronunciation.

EXERCISE 1

The underlined words in the sentences that follow are illiteracies (barbarisms). Rewrite each sentence, substituting the correct word for the wrong one.

a) There was a ghastly car accident that led to the dead of twenty people.

b) Scientists have proven the inexistence of aliens on this planet.

c) We had to pay R200 each for the obtention of a visa into Swaziland.

d) What your wife did is an unexcusable offence.

e) AIDS is an uncurable disease.

f) Oftenly, it is said that ignorancy is no excuse in a court of law.

g) Lettie cannot stand her boyfriend's jealousness.

h) The WHO recommends family planification as a birth control strategy.

i) What the minister said at the conference was unprecise.

j) This boy has pregnated his girlfriend.

EXERCISE 2

Rewrite the following passage, replacing all words that smack of illiteracy.

These nowadays, teenagers are no longer interesting in studies. There is so many attractions out there to busy them. I find this rather inacceptable because many parents go to all lengths to ensure a better feature for their offsprings who do not want to do anything else but enjoy theirselves. I feel that it is high time these kids listen to parental advices and stop making a fool of theirselves. They have to start doing something to better their lifes.

EXERCISE 3

Some errors stamp speakers or writers as illiterate. Such is the case with the following sentences. Correct them.

a) If we could drive like you do we would have arrived much earlier.

b) In response to same, I wish to inform you that the debt has been settled.

c) A person feels intimidated when closely observed.

d) Her performance was very unique this time around.

e) You often commit these errors. You must try to correct it.

f) I believe this is all right for now.

g) I hate these sort of trick.

h) Do you think that is worthwhile doing?

i) Due to unemployment, our compatriots are emigrating.

j) Your answer is almost quite correct.

Chapter 4

Capital Letters

This lesson dwells on the use of capital letters in the English language. Capital letters are required at the beginning of every sentence, sentences quoted in inverted commas, lines of poetry, proper nouns, adjectives formed from proper nouns, names of deities, important words in titles of books, plays, etc. You also have to use capital letters in days of the week, months of the year and special festivals (or events). Pronouns referring to God, Scriptures and theological works are generally written in capital letters.

Example 1
- Last Sunday, mafa and I went to the zion Christian church in moria. (*wrong*)
- Last Sunday, Mafa and I went to the Zion Christian Church in Moria. (*correct*)

Note the use of capital letters in Sunday, Mafa, I, Zion Christian, Church and Moria in sentence 2 above.

Example 2
- You said that there were two Ugandans and five nigerians in the african squad. (*wrong*)
- You said that there were two Ugandans and five Nigerians in the African Squad. (*correct*)

Note the use of capital letters in Ugandans, Nigerians and African in sentence two above. They are adjectives derived from proper nouns.

Example 3
- 'animal farm' is a political novel based on the russian revolution. (*wrong*) 'Animal Farm' is a political novel based on the Russian Revolution. (*correct*)

Note the use of capital letters in the book title "Animal Farm" and "Russian Revolution" (an important event in world history).

Example 4
- agnostics are people who believe that it is not possible to know whether god exists or not. (*wrong*)

- Agnostics are people who believe that it is not possible to know whether God exists or not. (*correct*)

Note the use of capital letters at the beginning of the sentence and in the word 'God' in sentence 2 above.

Example 5

- The manager said: 'remember, ladies and gentlemen, "The customer is always right" is a basic business precept.' (*wrong*)
- The manager said; 'Remember, ladies and gentlemen, "the customer is always right" is a basic business precept.' (*correct*)

Note the use of a capital letter in the word <u>Remember</u> and a small letter in the article <u>the</u> in sentence 2 above.

NOTE:

Capital letters should be used in the following instances:

1) At the beginning of every sentence;
2) At the beginning of sentences quoted in inverted commas;
3) At the beginning of each line of poetry, though modern poets often ignore this rule because of the well-known poetic licence;
4) With proper nouns;
5) With names of deities;
6) In all important words in titles of books;
7) In days of the weeks, months of the year, and special festivals or events;
8) With the personal pronoun (I) but not (me). Pronouns referring to God, the Scriptures, theological works, etc.
9) Adjectives formed from names of countries;
10) In the poetic device known as personification, when abstractions are referred to as people. E.g. To that high capital, where kingly Death /keep his pale court in beauty and decay, /He came.

EXERCISE 1

Insert capital letters where necessary in the sentences below.

a) jenny, would you please pass the salt over to me?
b) The roman catholic church frowns on polygamy.
c) John and helen live in pretoria.
d) The muslim feast of ramadan is celebrated every year.
e) I met a young belgian in festival street on tuesday. She was looking for union buildings.

f) Every june, we visit the kruger national park to watch wildlife.
g) My father once lived in paris, the french capital.
h) I once read a book titled: "to kill a man's pride."
i) It is said that chaka zulu was an indomitable warrior.
j) jesus christ was the son of god.

EXERCISE 2

Rewrite the following passage, substituting capital letters for small letters where necessary.

A TALE OF OUR TREE WORLD

My name is sam. i am ten years old. I like to be out in the veld, to sit on the soft green grass, and to listen to the beetles talking from the bark of trees: the buzz-buzz, sizzing-song that is their way of talking to one another. the woodpecker is here, making woody song right above me: tap, tap, tapping on the bark of a big branch looking for a meal of insects. sometimes he tap, tap, taps a hole in the branch to make a nest, a nice neat nest, to bring up his family. when i am out of doors in a green place i am so happy! i sit quietly, very quietly, watching the little people of the bush. the ants, they are always busy, going somewhere to find food, or taking care of their own large, very large family. the lizards slide and skate up and down the tree trunk and the rocks. they are a rock and bark colour---you can hardly see them. The spider, the lady spider is spinning her web in which she will catch her meal. the honey worker bees are flying from flower to flower looking for sweet nectar to suck up. (Written by *Sue Hart*)

Chapter 5

Circumlocution

This lesson pinpoints recurrent errors in English attributable to <u>circumlocution</u>. This linguistic term refers to the tendency to use <u>roundabout</u> expressions in communication. For example, the absence of noise is required of everyone who finds it necessary to work in the library.

There are instances when circumlocution is desirable in the interests of politeness, to avoid hurting others' sensibilities. In other words, by resorting to the use of circumlocution a speaker may convey an unpalatable idea in the least unsavoury way. On other occasions, directness and word economy are preferable.

Example 1
- The volcanologist pointed out that the eruption occurred since five years ago. (*verbose*)
- The volcanologist pointed out that the eruption occurred five years ago. (*correct*) **OR**
- The volcanologist pointed out that it is five years since the eruption occurred. (*correct*)

Example 2
- The orator said it made no difference <u>as far as</u> she was concerned. (*verbose*)
- The orator said it made no difference <u>to her</u>. (*correct*)

Example 3
- <u>As much as</u> I hate his arrogance, I value his erudition. (*verbose*)
- <u>Much as</u> I hate his arrogance, I value his erudition. (*correct*)

Notice that the as. as in sentence 1 above is redundant (unnecessary). The as. as construction implies comparison.

E.g The weather wasn't <u>as bad as</u> we thought.

Example 4
- Dr. Oupa Mashile advised me <u>as to how to</u> apply for a study grant. (*verbose*)
- Dr. Oupa Mashile advised me <u>how to</u> apply for a study grant. (*correct*)

The <u>as to</u> is often unwarranted in front of <u>why</u>, <u>whether</u>, <u>what</u>, <u>how</u>.

SAY: Information about my girlfriend's whereabouts. DON'T SAY: Information as to my girlfriend's whereabouts.

The golden rule of effective English is to say what one has to say in the fewest possible words. The most recurrent problem with contemporary speakers of English is the tendency to say what they have to say in as complicated a way as possible.

Instead of being simple and direct, communication is long-winded. This is because instead of choosing the simple word, communicators prefer the unusual. The purpose of communication is defeated if the reader has to pick his/her way.

Example 1
- A <u>very</u> good morning to you, Minister. (*wrong*)
- Good morning, Minister. (*correct*)

Many people would be hard pressed to explain the essence of the intensifier <u>very</u> in sentence 1 above. <u>Very</u> has lost its weight because of overuse by unthoughtful speakers.

Example 2
- South Africa is facing a <u>serious</u> moral crisis at the moment. (*wrong*)
- South Africa is facing a moral crisis at the moment. (*correct*)

Adjectives may act as meaningless intensifiers. It is important to ask yourself what precise meaning do they convey in the statement in which they appear. Look at sentence 1 above. Ask yourself what else is a crisis if it is not serious.

Example 3
- Our English language teacher gave us assignments with <u>monotonous</u> regularity. (*wrong*)
- Our English language teacher gave us assignments regularly. (*correct*)

The expression <u>monotonous</u> regularity is certainly tautological. What else is monotony if it is not regular?

Example 4
- Lazy students generally idle around <u>majority</u> of the time. (*wrong*)
- Lazy students generally idle around <u>most</u> of the time. (*correct*)

The word majority is best reserved for numbers, and not volume, amount or quantity. Use most or the greater part of in expressions having to do with time.

Example 5
- We are all aware of the press's fascination for the Queen. (*wrong*)
- We are all aware of the Queen's fascination for the press. (*correct*)

Fascination is the exercise (not the experience).

EXERCISE 1

Rewrite the following sentences, taking out all unnecessary words or expressions.

a) He is not so stupid as to think that some men are more superior to others.

b) As from Monday you will have to be punctual at work.

c) Paulette says that there was no doubt as to whether the earth was round.

d) Africa is hard hit by the AIDS pandemic at a time when most people are living in abject poverty.

e) I cannot give you a definite answer at this moment in time.

f) My younger brother joined the community police force on a voluntary basis.

g) My father lectures at UNISA on a part-time basis.

h) In the case of blind people, they may be taught by means of Braille.

i) In most cases, people ignore the importance of environmental care.

j) The price of petrol is higher than was the case last year.

EXERCISE 2

Correct errors of verbosity in the sentences below.

a) The general consensus is that most people are liars.

b) The policeman said the cause of the accident was due to drunkenness.

c) The boy wept because of the fact that his father had died.

d) The fact that the shop is closed means that we cannot buy some groceries.

e) I would be late for the meeting in view of the fact that I have a tyre puncture.
f) My uncle's car is red in colour.
g) Henry's room is rectangular in shape.
h) The crowd at the stadium is small in number.
i) Outside of the parking lot you'll find my bike.
j) This athlete is very tall in height.

Chapter 6

Clumsy Expressions

Some expressions used by speakers of English are clumsy and mar the correctness of thought in communication. The aim of this lesson is to pinpoint a couple of such expressions in a bid to remind users of English to be mindful when they communicate. The following examples would shed some light on the subject under discussion, namely the improper use of the following expressions: <u>the reason is because</u>, <u>quite unique</u>, <u>use to</u>.

Example 1
- The reason why Maria Mashilo phoned was <u>because</u> she was worried. (*wrong*)
- The reason Maria Mashilo phoned was <u>that</u> she was worried. (*correct*) **OR**
- Maria Mashilo phoned because she was worried. (correct) It is also wrong to say: the reason for the accident was due to speed.

SAY: The reason for the accident was speed. **OR** The accident was due to speed.

Example 2
- The culture of these people is <u>quite unique</u>. (*wrong*)
- The culture of these people is <u>unique</u>. (*correct*)

<u>Unique</u> means without equal. Something that is unique is the only one of its kind. It is an absolute. There can be no degree of uniqueness. Something is either unique or not. So <u>quite unique</u>, <u>rather unique</u>, <u>very unique</u>, etc. are illogical and ungrammatical expressions. You shouldn't blur the uniqueness of unique by qualifying it in any way.

Example 3
- Trudi <u>use to</u> accompany me to SUPEDI in Seshego. (*wrong*)
- Trudi <u>used to</u> accompany me to SUPEDI in Seshego. (*correct*)

<u>Used to</u> and <u>use to</u> are often confused because they sound alike. The adjectival form <u>used to</u> means <u>accustomed to</u>. Use to is the infinitive form used after did. For example, did you use to play badminton?

In this lesson, I shall endeavour to correct some clumsy sentences that I have picked up in the conversation of students. Most of these errors stem from misplaced words.

Example 1
- A girl has a car who is in our class. (*wrong*)
- A girl who has a car is in our class. (*correct*)

The relative clause must be put immediately after the noun to which it refers. "Who has a car" refers to "girl" and should come immediately after it.

Example 2
- He neither speaks Afrikaans nor Sepedi. (*wrong*)
- He speaks neither Afrikaans nor Sepedi. (*correct*) Correlative conjunctions (that is, conjunctions used in pairs, like either - or, neither - nor, not only - but also, etc.), should be placed before words of the same part of speech.

Example 3
- Chueu said she had never met a such good man before. (*wrong*)
- Chueu said she had never met such a good man before. (*correct*) **OR**
- Chueu said she had never met so good a man before. (*correct*)

The indefinite article "a" or "an" should come after "such" and "so," as seen in sentence 2 and 3 above.

Example 4
- Only I and my brother were present at the fundraiser. (*wrong*)
- Only my brother and I were present at the fundraiser. (*correct*)

English idiom requires that when a person is speaking of himself/herself and others, (s)he must mention other persons first. But, in confessing a fault, the English idiom requires that the speaker should mention himself/herself first. For instance, I and my brother broke the window.

Example 5
- Why you were absent from school yesterday, Sipho? (*wrong*)
- Why were you absent from school yesterday, Sipho? (*correct*)

In interrogative sentences beginning with words like what, when, why and how, the verb is generally placed before the subject as seen in sentence 2 above.

Example 6
- Kupa wrote <u>carefully</u> his matric exam. (*wrong*)
- Kupa wrote his matric exam <u>carefully</u>. (*correct*)

With a transitive verb, the adverb usually comes after the object as in sentence 2 above.

This lesson tackles some common mistakes made by speakers of English who claim that they have been hearing the expression for a long time. Many people feel that because they have heard something said very often and over a long period of time, it must therefore be correct. This, of course, is quite untrue. My elementary school teacher spent seven years telling me to draw a round circle! Of course, he was not correct. In a great many cases, it is very difficult for a teacher to convince students that common expressions they have grown up with over the years are in fact, quite incorrect grammar and bad English.

Look at the following examples.

Example 1
- This is my first time of <u>coming</u> here. (*wrong*)
- This is the first time that I <u>have been</u> here. (*correct*)

The first sentence is wrong because the present continuous tense 'coming' is not acceptable in this circumstance.

Example 2
- She said it was her first time of <u>seeing</u> that. (*wrong*)
- She said it was the first time she <u>had seen</u> that. (*correct*) Once again, the first sentence is incorrect because of the misuse of the present continuous tense (i.e. seeing).

Example 3
- This is my very first time of <u>witnessing</u> an accident of this nature. (*wrong*)
- This is the very first time I <u>have witnessed</u> an accident of this nature. (*correct*)

It is important to draw readers' attention to the substitution of the definite article 'the' for the possessive pronouns in the wrong sentences above.

Example 4
- I am sick since last week Thursday. (*wrong*)
- I <u>have been</u> sick since last Thursday. (*correct*)

This statement is made by someone who wants to tell us that last Thursday (s)he became sick and is still sick at the time of speaking. The sentence should be in the present perfect tense, which is the tense used to connect something that was started in the past and is still going on at the time of speech.

Example 5
- I am coming with the bus to school this morning. (*wrong*)
- I came by bus to school this morning. (*correct*)

There is often great confusion in the use of gerunds and prepositions in connection with travel. Don't say: I came by foot. Say: I came on foot. Don't say: I came on bicycle. Say: I came by bicycle.

In the course of this lesson, we shall revisit some recurrent problems in written and spoken English stemming from the improper use of the following expressions: on account of, suffering with, no sooner when, more preferable.

Example 1
- Maria Mafokoane stayed at home on account of she was feeling ill. (*wrong*)
- Maria Mafokoane stayed at home on account of feeling ill. (*correct*) **OR**
- Maria Mafokoane stayed at home because she was feeling ill. (*correct*)

Example 2
- No sooner had the kwaito band started to play when the lights went off. (*wrong*)
- No sooner had the kwaito band started to play than the lights went off. (*correct*)

No sooner should be followed by than, not when or that.

Example 3
- The match had hardly started than hooligans took the stadium by storm. (*wrong*)
- The match had hardly started when hooligans took the stadium by storm. (*correct*)

Hardly should be followed by when, not than, when the sense is no sooner.

Example 4
- Mrs. Nobody who was <u>suffering with</u> pneumonia died yesterday. (*wrong*)
- Mrs. Nobody who was <u>suffering from</u> pneumonia died yesterday. (*correct*)

<u>Suffering with</u> is colloquial English. Use <u>suffer from</u> which is conventional.

Example 5
- An evening with Sandra is <u>more preferable than</u> staying at home. (*wrong*)
- An evening with Sandra is <u>preferable to</u> staying at home. (*correct*)

The word <u>preferable</u> collocates with <u>than</u> and must not be qualified.

This lesson focuses on the incorrect use of some words and expressions in the English language. Words and expressions such as: <u>both, comprise, can't, much less, centre on</u> do pose quite a few communication problems to non-native speakers of English.

Example 1
- The journey to Tzaneen was <u>both</u> long, boring and exhausting. (*wrong*)
- The journey to Tzaneen was long, boring and exhausting. (*correct*)

The word <u>both</u> should not be used for more than two persons or things as seen in sentence 1 above.

Example 2
- The discussion of the Asian tourists <u>centred round</u> the rich cultural heritage of South Africa. (*wrong*)
- The discussion of the Asian tourists <u>centred on</u> the rich cultural heritage of South Africa. (*correct*)

A discussion may <u>centre on</u> a subject or <u>revolve around</u> it, but not <u>centre round</u> it.

Example 3
- I <u>can't seem</u> to understand what's wrong with teenagers of today. (*wrong*)

- I am <u>unable</u> to understand what's wrong with teenagers of today. (*correct*) **OR**
- I <u>seem unable</u> to understand what's wrong with teenagers of today. (*correct*)

Example 4
- The Legislature <u>comprises of</u> the National Council of Provinces and the Parliament. (*wrong*)
- The Legislature <u>comprises</u> the National Council of Provinces and the Parliament. (*correct*) **OR**
- The Legislature <u>consists of</u> (<u>is composed of</u>) the National Council of Provinces and the Parliament. (*correct*)

More often than not, clumsy sentence structure stems from the overuse of colloquialisms and slang. In formal writing these expressions should be avoided. In a similar vein, communicators should endeavour to keep away from clichés (hackneyed or overused expressions). What you say or write should immediately bring a picture to mind. If you can convey a precise image or an emotion that you feel to another person in writing, then it is good style.

A colloquialism is the kind of slang that is peculiar to an area or the dialect of a given linguistic community. It is not correct grammar. Clichés are used in daily conversation, often with sickening repetition.

Example 1
- The trade union leader was <u>conspicuous by his absence</u>. (*cliché*)
- The trade union leader was <u>conspicuously absent</u>. **OR**
- The trade union leader was <u>remarkably</u> absent.

Example 2
- <u>By and large</u>, the media view the proposed Curriculum 21 with a certain degree of skepticism. (*cliché*)
- <u>In sum</u>, the media view the proposed Curriculum 21 with a certain degree of skepticism.

Example 3
- <u>To all intents and purposes</u>, she is my mother. (*cliché*)
- <u>All the same</u> she is my mother.

Example 4
- The pursuit of fairness is the <u>acid test</u> of democracy. (*cliché*)

- The pursuit of fairness is the <u>true test</u> of democracy.

Example 5
- I met this <u>bloke</u> five years ago in London. (*cliché*)
- I met this <u>man</u> five years ago in London.

Example 6
- My teacher is a real <u>cool dude</u>. (*cliché*)
- My teacher is a real <u>nice man</u>.

In daily conversation, it may be desirable to depart from the formal forms of expressions and use colloquialisms, clichés, slangs and idioms. But this must be done sparingly.

EXERCISE 1
Correct the following badly written sentences.
a) Peter's apartment's window has been broken by thieves.
b) Mary's husband is taller than me.
c) There is no point in me begging her to marry me.
d) I believe it was him who raped the student.
e) A family friend of him had an accident with his bike.
f) Blackie and myself will not be present at the meeting.
g) Doctor Khumalo plays a good play.
h) The four pupils started to kick themselves.
i) This is the worst march that I have never seen.
j) My friend wears the same jacket that I wear.

EXERCISE 2
Rewrite the following sentences correcting all wrong expressions.
a) Nelson is a man who every one can trust.
b) Please tell Susan to give me one another novel, I don't like this one.
c) I believe that one should spend his money judiciously.
d) Whom of the two players is better?
e) The three sisters helped each other.
f) Being in haste the car keys were forgotten.
g) If John would do us this favour, we shall be thankful.
h) According to our opinion, we think that a teacher is never wrong.

i) School starts at eight and a half o'clock every day from Monday to Friday.

j) At the end the tourists reached the top of the peak.

Chapter 7

Collocation

In this lesson, we shall focus attention on common errors in spoken and written English associated with wrong 'collocation.' Collocation is the way in which some words occur regularly whenever another word is used. This is a technical term in linguistics. English collocational errors are quite rampant in English verbal idioms. An idiom is a group of words which have a different meaning when used together from the one they would have if you took the meaning of each word individually. It is the kind of language that people use at a particular time or in a particular setting. We shall provide some examples to make this point clear to users of English.

Example 1

- Having made your decisions you should <u>abide to</u> them. (*wrong*)
- Having made your decisions you should <u>abide by</u> them. (*correct*)

The first sentence is wrong because of incorrect collocation (i.e. abide to). 'Abide by' is an English idiomatic expression that does not allow for alteration. If you abide by a law, rule, agreement or decision, you do what it says you should do.

Notice that you also '<u>abide by a promise</u>.'

Example 2

- In our teens, our father did not <u>approve</u> our going to nightclubs. (*wrong*)
- In our teens, our father did not <u>approve of</u> our going to nightclubs. (*correct*)

The first sentence is incorrect because the speaker has omitted the preposition 'of' which collocates with the verb 'approve.' To <u>approve of</u> something means 'regard that thing with favour.' Note, however, that <u>to approve</u> is acceptable English if you meant to say 'give consent to,' for example, <u>approve the commencement of work on a project</u>.

Example 3
- I shall avail myself <u>to</u> every opportunity of travelling overseas. (*wrong*)
- I shall avail myself <u>of</u> every opportunity of travelling overseas. (*correct*)

Note that the collocation between the verb 'avail' and the preposition 'to' in the first sentence is unacceptable. 'Avail oneself of' something is an idiomatic way of saying 'make use of' or 'take advantage of.'

Example 4
- A noisy home environment is not <u>conducive for</u> reading. (*wrong*)
- A noisy home environment is not <u>conducive to</u> reading. (*correct*)

Notice that the collocation between the adjective 'conducive' and the preposition 'for' in the first sentence is unacceptable. Conducive always takes <u>to</u>. If an environment is 'conducive to reading,' it is <u>suitable</u> for reading. Notice that the adjective 'suitable' collocates with 'for.'

Example 5
- The terms of the contract have now been <u>agreed with</u>. (*wrong*)
- The terms of contract have now been <u>agreed to</u>. (*correct*) Note that 'agreed with' cannot be used in the <u>passive</u> form. That's why the first sentence is wrong. Conversely, it is acceptable to use 'agreed to' in the passive as seen in the second sentence.

It is important to stress that the use of the passive form without the preposition has gained currency over the past few years.

Thus, 'terms of the contract have now been agreed' is correct usage.

EXERCISE 1
Some expressions collocate with specific prepositions in English. Fill in the preposition that collocates most appropriately with the verbs in the following sentences.
a) Thiza was fined_____speeding last weekend.
b) The street kids got used_____sleeping in the open air.
c) You do this task_____own risk.

d) Miranda succeeded____convincing him to marry her.
e) I look forward_seeing both of you at the workshop.
f) Salome is good mimicking people who stammer.
g) I have great pleasure__informing you that I passed my examination with five distinctions.
h) I read newspapers in order____improve on my communication skills.
i) Nana was praised____her excellent performance at the competition.
j) Are you still keen____joining the newly-formed Democratic Alliance Party?

EXERCISE 2

Complete the following sentences by writing a suitable word in the blank spaces.

a) Let me warn you that this is no time__jokes.
b) I prefer reading_____drinking liquor all the time.
c) She is an authority____gender issues.
d) I am very sensitive____abusive language.
e) There is no means____finding out the truth about the relationship between HIV and AIDS.
f) Msimang had the privilege____being the guest_____ honour at the function.
g) Your comportment leaves much_____be desired.
h) He arrived at the airport_____the nick of time.
i) South Africa was disqualified__hosting the 2006 Soccer World Cup.
j) William van Breda is good____cooking the books.

Chapter 8

Comparatives and Superlatives

This lesson focuses on common errors in English stemming from the misuse of the <u>comparative</u> and <u>superlative</u> forms of adjectives. To begin with, I would like to emphasize that there are <u>three</u> degrees of comparison in English (positive / comparative / superlative), e.g. good - better - best / big - bigger- biggest / beautiful - <u>more</u> beautiful - <u>most</u> beautiful, etc.

Example 1
- James is the <u>tallest</u> of the twin brothers. *(wrong)*
- James is the <u>taller</u> of the twin brothers. *(correct)*

When only <u>two</u> things or persons are compared, the <u>comparative</u> must be used. Twins are <u>two persons</u>, therefore, the comparative form should be used.

Example 2
- Susan is the <u>more unfortunate</u> of the five accident victims. *(wrong)*
- Susan is the <u>most unfortunate</u> of the five accident victims. *(correct)*

When more than two persons or things are being compared, the <u>superlative</u> must be used. In the example above, there are five accident victims. This is why the adjective <u>unfortunate</u> should be preceded by <u>most</u> instead of <u>more</u>.

Example 3
- Kenyan sprinters are <u>more</u> faster than other African short-distance runners. *(wrong)*
- Kenyan sprinters are <u>faster</u> than other African short-distance runners. *(correct)*

The use of the <u>double comparative</u> in the first sentence is ungrammatical. As a general rule, monosyllabic words (= words with one sound segment) are not preceded by <u>more</u> or <u>most</u>.

They take the <u>er</u> and <u>est</u> suffixes in the <u>comparative</u> and <u>superlative</u> forms. However, there are a few exceptions to this rule which shall be discussed in subsequent lessons.

Example 4
- Uncle Jack's car is <u>more better</u> than my dad's. *(wrong)*
- Uncle Jack's car is <u>better</u> than my dad's. *(correct)*

Once again, the use of the double comparative more <u>better</u> makes the first sentence incorrect. Note that the adjectives good and <u>bad</u> have irregular forms of comparison: <u>good</u> - <u>better</u> - <u>best</u>/ <u>bad</u> - <u>worse</u> - <u>worst</u>.

Example 5
- <u>More people</u> will agree with me that this is a corrupt society. *(wrong)*
- <u>Most people</u> will agree with me that this is a corrupt society. *(correct)*

The word <u>most</u> should be used when 'the majority of' is implied. This is what the speaker intended to say in the first sentence: <u>the majority of people would agree with me that this is a corrupt society</u>.

Example 6
- She is one of the <u>good</u> girls I have ever met. *(wrong)*
- She is one of the <u>best</u> girls I have ever met. *(correct)*

It is correct to use the superlative <u>best</u> because the speaker implies <u>one among many</u> girls.

The aim of this lesson is to discuss the use of the <u>comparative</u> and <u>superlative</u> forms of adjectives in the English language. The difference between big / bigger / biggest is that bigger indicates a higher degree of the quantity of being <u>big</u> and biggest indicates the highest degree. The <u>er</u> form is called the comparative and the <u>est</u> form is known as the superlative. Longer adjectives and adverbs form the comparative and superlative by having <u>more</u> and <u>most</u> placed before them.

Some adjectives have two comparative and two superlative forms (e.g. lovely - lovelier - loveliest **OR** lovely - more lovely - most lovely).

Example 1
- This is the <u>most latest</u> fashion design on the market. *(wrong)*
- This is the <u>latest</u> fashion design on the market. *(correct)* Care should be taken to avoid the use of double comparatives and superlatives because they cloud meaning.

Example 2
- Ballistic missiles are more lethal than any weapons of mass destruction. (*wrong*)
- Ballistic missiles are more lethal than other weapons of mass destruction. (*correct*)

Sentence 1 gives the impression that ballistic missiles are not weapons of war. Care should be taken not to compare things which belong in the same class.

Example 3
- Lettie doesn't want none of these posters. (*wrong*)
- Lettie doesn't want any of these posters. (*correct*) **OR**
- Lettie wants none of these posters. (*correct*)

Two negative modifiers cancel each other out. Consequently, sentence 1 translates as: Lettie wants some of these posters.

Example 4
- This educator doesn't know nothing about outcomes-based education. (*wrong*)
- This educator knows nothing about outcomes-based education. (*correct*) **OR**
- This educator doesn't know anything about outcomes-based education. (*correct*)

Double negatives may have a shed of meaning but an overuse of this device may lead to ambiguity.

EXERCISE 1
Give the correct form of the adjective enclosed in brackets.
a) Larry Stengard is the (sinful) of the three men.
b) Khosi is the (cruel) of the five criminals.
c) Bridget is the (tactless) of the four leaders.
d) Euthanasia is the (brutal) of the two types of crimes.
e) Irene Aphane is (afraid) than her opponent.
f) Arnold is (ill) today than yesterday.
g) Maryke is the (sly) of all the politicians.
h) Moyo's article is the (sordid) I ever read.
i) We live in the (appalling) conditions.
j) Rebone is the (shy) of all my children.

EXERCISE 2
Write down the correct form of the word in brackets.
a) Tanya did (badly) than Tselane.
b) Maitland was (annoyed) than the others.
c) Tsidi is the (talented) of the three singers.
d) Choh ran (fast) than Bala in the race.
e) Susungi moved (slowly) than Abe.
f) Lou talks (loudly) than Echaw.
g) We will know the truth (soon) rather than (late).
h) He left the hall (hastily) than expected.
i) Please talk to me in a (aggressive) manner.
j) Local folks are sometimes (vocal) than expected.

EXERCISE 3
Rewrite the following sentences, putting the adjectives in the appropriate degree of comparison.
a) Lilly is the (strong) girl in the school.
b) James is the (handsome) of the two brothers.
c) Sue is the (young) of all twenty athletes.
d) Jill is the (old) of all the ten boxers.
e) Yours is the (good) story so far.
f) Which of the two do you like (much), tea or coffee?
g) Gold is the (expensive) of the precious stones.
h) The Zambezi is the (long) river in this part of Africa.
i) Georgette is (bad) than her sister.
j) Which of the six trees is the (tall)?

Chapter 9

Concord

In this lesson, we shall focus attention on the agreement between verbs and their subjects in <u>number</u> and <u>person</u>. This aspect of English grammar is called <u>concord</u>. Whether you are a matriculant or a standard six (grade 8) pupil, you need to master the correct usage of concord in order to write clearly. The following examples illustrate the point.

<u>Some singular nouns combined to form one idea with a singular meaning, require a singular verb</u>; bread and butter, steak and onions, brandy and water, toast and butter, etc. Whenever any of the above-mentioned combinations is used as the subject of a sentence, it is necessary that they be followed or preceded by a singular verb.

Example 1
- <u>Were</u> the <u>bread and butter</u> on the table? (*wrong*)
- <u>Was</u> the <u>bread and butter</u> on the table? (*correct*)
- <u>Steak and onions are</u> all you get for lunch. (*wrong*)
- <u>Steak and onions is</u> all you get for lunch. (*correct*)

<u>Some nouns that look plural have a singular meaning and take singular verbs</u>. E.g. News, means, whereabouts, etc.

Example 2
- <u>Were</u> the <u>news</u> that she received good or bad? (*wrong*)
- <u>Was</u> the <u>news</u> that she received good or bad? (*correct*)

Example 3
- My friend's <u>whereabouts are</u> unknown. (*wrong*)
- My friend's <u>whereabouts is</u> unknown. (*correct*)

<u>A pair of items generally requires a singular verb</u>. For example, a pair of scissors, a pair of pliers, a pair of trousers, a pair of glasses, a pair of compasses, etc.

Example 4
- His pair of glasses <u>were</u> lying on the coffee-table. (*wrong*)
- His pair of glasses <u>was</u> lying on the coffee-table. (*correct*)

Pupils should note, however, that when words like <u>trousers</u>, <u>pants</u>, <u>shorts</u>, <u>pyjamas</u>, <u>scissors</u>, <u>spectacles</u>, <u>compasses</u>, etc. are used on their own without the phrase "a pair of" they require plural verbs. E.g. Your trousers <u>are</u> dirty, your shorts <u>are</u> immaculate, etc.

When two subjects are joined by conjunctival phrases (e.g. <u>as well as</u>, <u>together with</u>, <u>including</u>, etc.), the verb agrees with the subject that stands first.

Example 5
- Harry <u>as well as</u> his cousins <u>were</u> invited to Jeanne's birthday party. (*wrong*)
- Harry <u>as well as</u> his cousins <u>was</u> invited to Jeanne's birthday party. (*correct*)
- The bitch, <u>together with</u> ten puppies <u>were</u> shot by the mad man. (*wrong*)
- The bitch, <u>together with</u> ten puppies, <u>was</u> shot by the mad man. (*correct*)

Achieving concord (agreement) between verbs and plural/singular nouns often poses huge problems to non-native speakers of English. In this lesson, I will pinpoint some rampant cases of wrong concord and suggest solutions.

Example 1
- The mineworker deserted his post because his <u>wage</u> was low. (*wrong*)
- The mineworker deserted his post because his wages <u>were</u> low. (*correct*)

<u>Wages</u> is a plural noun and takes a plural verb. But we say a <u>living wage</u>.

Example 2
- The Bible says that <u>riches is</u> the root of all evil. (*wrong*)
- The Bible says that <u>riches are</u> the root of all evil. (*correct*) It is noteworthy that <u>riches</u> is a plural noun and always takes a plural verb as seen in sentence 2 above.

Example 3
- Modern farmers are using new <u>machineries</u>. (*wrong*)
- Modern farmers are using new <u>machinery</u>. (*correct*) Notice that <u>machinery</u> is a singular noun and always takes a singular verb. But we say a <u>piece of machinery</u> or <u>pieces of</u> <u>machinery</u>.

Example 4
- We were glad to hear that the news <u>were</u> good. (*wrong*)

- We were glad to hear that the news <u>was</u> good. (*correct*)

It bears emphasizing that though plural in form, <u>news</u> always takes a singular verb. If only one thing is meant, we say <u>a piece of news</u> or <u>an item of news</u>. For example, <u>this is a good piece of news</u> for rape victims.

Example 5
- For fear of robbery, Mr. Mbuli keeps all his <u>monies</u> in the bank. (*wrong*)
- For fear of robbery, Mr. Mbuli keeps all his <u>money</u> in the bank. (*correct*)
- Money is a singular noun and always takes a singular verb. However, <u>monies</u> is used to refer to several separate sums of money that form part of a larger amount that is received or spent. For example, the investment and management of <u>monies</u> by pension funds.

In today's lesson, we shall revisit <u>concord</u> (i.e. agreement between a verb and its subject in number and person) in English grammar. Concord is such a slippery aspect of the English language that speakers need to devote considerable time to its full mastery.

Alternative subjects joined by "or" or "nor"

When alternative subjects are joined by the words "or" or "nor," the verb agrees with the nearer one.

Example 1
- Either John or his sisters <u>is</u> lying. (*wrong*)
- Either John or his sisters <u>are</u> lying. (*correct*)
- Neither he nor they <u>is</u> angry. (*wrong*)
- Neither he nor they <u>are</u> angry. (*correct*)

The relative pronoun "who" preceded by an antecedent The relative pronoun "who" serves as a plural subject when its antecedent (word that comes before) is plural.

Example 2
- He is not one of those <u>who thinks</u> they are superior. (*wrong*)
- He is not one of those <u>who think</u> they are superior. (*correct*)
- She is one of those women <u>who believes</u> in female empowerment. (*wrong*)
- She is one of those women <u>who believe</u> in female empowerment. (*correct*)

A fraction of a collective noun is considered a singular subject

Example 3
- Two-thirds of the farm <u>are</u> fertile. (*wrong*)
- Two-thirds of the farm <u>is</u> fertile. (*correct*)

A fraction of a countable plural noun is regarded as a plural subject

Example 4
- Two-thirds of the animals <u>is</u> dead. (*wrong*)
- Two-thirds of the animals <u>are</u> dead. (*correct*)
- Three-quarters of the pupils <u>has</u> fallen pregnant. (*wrong*)
- Three-quarters of the pupils <u>have</u> fallen pregnant. (*correct*)

The singular noun "nothing" as a subject

The verb agrees with the singular noun "nothing" when it serves as the subject of a sentence.

Example 5
- Nothing but wild fruits <u>were</u> eaten by the travelers. (*wrong*)
- Nothing but wild fruits <u>was</u> eaten by the travelers. (*correct*)
- Nothing but oats <u>are</u> sown here. (*wrong*)
- Nothing but oats <u>is</u> sown here. (*correct*)

A group of words conveying the idea of oneness

A group of words conveying the idea of <u>oneness</u> may take either the singular or plural verb depending on the speaker's focus.

Example 6
- The <u>committee is</u> sitting today. (focus on the collectivity)
- The <u>committee are</u> sitting today. (focus on individual members of the committee)
- The <u>government has</u> not fulfilled <u>its</u> election promises. (focus on the collectivity)
- The <u>government have</u> not fulfilled <u>their</u> election promises. (focus on individual arms of government)

Errors stemming from non-agreement of verbs in number are frequent in the exam scripts that we mark year in and year out. Teachers encounter similar problems in the classwork and assignments submitted by pupils. We have to spot these problems and correct them before they become part of the learner's speech pattern.

Example 1
- The principal announced that a large <u>supply</u> of books <u>were</u> expected for the forthcoming school year. (*wrong*)
- The principal announced that a large <u>supply</u> of books <u>was</u> expected for the forthcoming school year. (*correct*)

When the subject is singular, the verb must be singular, and when the subject is plural, the verb must be plural as well. Care should be taken when a plural noun (e.g. books) comes between a singular subject (e.g. <u>supply</u>) and its verb. The subject of this sentence is <u>supply</u>, and not <u>books</u>.

Example 2
- Many teenagers lost their <u>life</u> while swimming at sea. (*wrong*)
- Many teenagers lost their <u>lives</u> while swimming at sea. (*correct*)

In English, words such as <u>life</u>, <u>heart</u>, <u>soul</u>, <u>body</u> and <u>mind</u>, are used in the plural form when they refer to more than one person.

Example 3
- Doctor Khumalo does not play soccer <u>like</u> I do. (*wrong*)
- Doctor Khumalo does not play soccer <u>as</u> I do. (*correct*) <u>As</u> is a conjunction, and is usually followed by a noun or pronoun in the nominative case.

Example 4
- <u>This</u> errors are made by foreigners learning to speak our native tongue. (*wrong*)
- <u>These</u> errors are made by foreigners learning to speak our native tongue. (*correct*)

<u>This</u> changes to <u>these</u> if the noun that follows is in the plural number as seen in the sentences above.

Example 5
- There <u>is</u> many pupils waiting to talk to the principal. (*wrong*)
- There <u>are</u> many pupils waiting to talk to the principal. (*correct*)

<u>There is</u> changes to <u>there are</u> if the noun that follows is in the plural number.

EXERCISE 1
Choose the correct verb from the pairs provided.
a) (Is/Are) bread and cheese on the table?
b) (Was/Were) the bread and jam eaten?

c) The news (was/were) shocking.
d) The council (has/have) published the annual report.
e) The board (is/are) sitting today.
f) Mpho's pants (are/is) torn in the right leg.
g) She went to fetch a pair of pliers that (was/were) in the cupboard.
h) One of the women (was/were) guilty.
i) A range of goods (was/were) bought from Sunnypark.
j) All along the road (lies/lie) traces of blood.

EXERCISE 2

Fill each blank space with the correct verb chosen from the pair in brackets.

a) Joseph is one of those who___(thinks/think) so much about riches.
b) Mathematics___(is/are) my favourite subject at school.
c) Jonas or Sedibana____(is/are) leaving for overseas tomorrow.
d) Either he or she_____(is/are) wrong.
e) Not only I but also they_____(am/are) right.
f) Liza as well as her brothers___(was/were) invited for dinner.
g) Many a tourist_(has/have) been killed in this country.
h) Three-quarters of the farm___(is/are) arid.
i) Nothing but protea___(grow/grows) here.
j) Their aim and objective_____(is/are) to make progress.

EXERCISE 3

Select the appropriate verb from the pair in brackets.

a) Sports (is/are) necessary for a healthy body.
b) This series of articles (is/are) quite informative.
c) Three hours' play (was/were) enough for me.
d) There (has/have) been one or two volcanic eruptions this year.
e) A minimum of fifty credits (is/are) required to be admitted to sit the examination.
f) Two-thirds of the animals (were/was) killed by the tornado.
g) The corps of soldiers (was/were) victorious.

h) The greater part of those three weeks of vacation (was/were) spent at the Kruger National Park.
i) The committee (has/have) arrived at a consensus.
j) A mob of vagrants (has/have) taken the city by storm.

Chapter 10

Determiners

This lesson is aimed at shedding some light on the correct use of general determiners in the English language. Quantities and amounts of things are often referred to using numbers. You can use general determiners such as <u>some,</u> <u>any,</u> <u>all,</u> <u>every</u> and <u>much</u> to talk about quantities and amounts of things. It bears emphasizing that there are restrictions on using <u>much</u> in positive statements as seen in the examples below.

Example 1
- I enjoyed <u>very much</u> the party. (*wrong*)
- I enjoyed the party <u>very much</u>. (*correct*)

When <u>very much</u> is used with a transitive verb as seen above, it is usually placed after the object as seen in sentence 2 above.

Example 2
- I enjoyed the gala evening <u>much</u>. (*wrong*)
- I enjoyed the gala evening <u>very much</u>. (*correct*)

In positive sentences, like the ones above, you do not use <u>much</u> without <u>very</u>. In negative sentences, you may use <u>much</u> without <u>very</u>. It is correct to say '<u>Sanah didn't like him much</u>' or 'The <u>situation isn't likely to change much</u>.'

Example 3
- William Morudu knows <u>much</u> about safe sex. (*wrong*)
- William Morudu knows <u>a lot</u> about safe sex. (*correct*) Notice that you do not use <u>much</u> as an object pronoun in positive sentences. Instead you use <u>a lot</u>. You say 'He knows <u>a lot</u> about drugs'/ 'I think she knows <u>a lot</u> about men.'

Example 4
- The <u>amount</u> of people who pay their TV license in this country is insignificant. (*wrong*)
- The <u>number</u> of people who pay their TV license in this country is insignificant. (*correct*)

Note that you do not talk about an <u>amount</u> of things or people. For example, you do not say 'There was an amount of tables missing from the hall.' You say 'There was a number of tables missing from the hall.'

Note also that when you use <u>amount</u> in the plural, you must use a plural verb with it. It is incorrect to say 'large <u>amounts</u> of money <u>was</u> spent on the project.' You say 'large amounts of money <u>were</u> spent on the project.'

Example 5
- The weatherman said it was <u>less cold than</u> it was yesterday. (*wrong*)
- The weatherman said it was <u>not as cold as</u> it was yesterday. (*correct*)

In conversation, people do not usually use <u>less</u> in front of adjectives as seen in sentence 1 above.

EXERCISE 1

Rewrite each of the following sentences using an acceptable determiner in the place of the underlined words.

a) Barry will have to bring <u>another</u> money in order to complete his payment for the car.

b) Brownwell invited all his friends to a birthday party but <u>a few</u> came.

c) Do you like milk in your coffee, Brendan? Yes, just <u>little</u>.

d) Donald Cook gave Hubert a strong cup of coffee, saying that there was <u>a little</u> milk left.

e) Wallmach complained that the <u>whole</u> clothes had been stolen.

f) The <u>entire</u> streets in Hammanskraal have potholes.

g) <u>All</u> the street was flooded after the downpour.

h) Kim stressed that a caring mother wouldn't hit <u>some</u> of her children.

i) Whenever Johan enters <u>any</u> shop, he buys something.

j) Coetzee has eaten the <u>whole</u> of the cake.

EXERCISE 2

Rewrite the following sentences correctly.

a) Tepla thinks that there is no any restaurant in Messina.

b) "That's all; I have no any other point to make," said the minister.

c) Katz told me that the actresses taking part in the play were four.

d) Horton feels that we must find other two colours to match these two.

e) Brandon said that more fifty pupils were admitted into their school at the end of last term.

f) McCarron says you are making too much of noise in this room.

g) It gives me much of pleasure to be given this opportunity to address you this evening.

h) Dubois spends a large part of her time signing documents.

i) Matthew Weir pointed out that there is plenty rich land in his village.

J) Gunter was detained, the rest offenders were set free.

EXERCISE 3

Use **many** or **much** in the sentences that follow.

a) Mary hasn't____food left.
b) Are there_____clothes in the wardrobe?
c) There isn't____money available, my boy.
d) Does Benny take_____interest in sport?
e) Manu hasn't___time left.
f) Dudu tells me there are so____students in class?
g) How__people are absent today?
h) There hasn't been____sunshine these days.
i) He doesn't know_____French.
j) _____ drops of water can fill a bucket.

Chapter 11

Gerunds

In this lesson, I would like to discuss common errors in written and spoken English associated with the incorrect use of gerunds in combination with pronouns. When we use a <u>gerund</u> as the subject of a sentence, it should be preceded by a <u>possessive adjective</u> and not by a <u>pronoun</u>. Look at the following examples:

Example 1
- <u>You</u> coming in late every night annoys everyone in this house. (*wrong*)
- <u>Your</u> coming in late every night annoys everyone in this house. (*correct*)

The first sentence is incorrect because the gerund 'coming' is preceded by a pronoun 'you' and not by a possessive adjective 'your' as shown in the second sentence.

Example 2
- The accident was the result of <u>him driving</u> too fast. (*wrong*)
- The accident was the result of <u>his driving</u> too fast. (*correct*) The first sentence is wrong because the word 'driving' is used as a gerund or verbal noun and should be preceded by a possessive adjective rather than a pronoun.

Example 3
- I dislike <u>you</u> when you are smoking. (*wrong*)
- I dislike <u>your</u> smoking. (*correct*)

The first sentence means that you dislike the person when he is in the act of smoking. Here, 'smoking' is a present participle and part of the present continuous tense of the verb 'to smoke.' But if you say: 'I dislike your smoking,' it means you dislike the action of smoking. Here 'smoking' is used as a gerund and therefore should be preceded by the possessive adjective 'your.'

Example 4
- <u>They roaming</u> the streets at midnight annoys their mother. (*wrong*)

- Their roaming the streets at midnight annoys their mother.

(*correct*)

The first sentence is incorrect because the gerund 'roaming' is used as the subject of the sentence, and should be preceded by the possessive adjective 'their.'

The use of gerunds or verbal nouns often causes great confusion. Teachers and users of English should pay extra attention to this aspect of grammar.

EXERCISE 1

Gerunds end in -ing but act as nouns. When qualified they must be preceded by an adjective. Correct the sentences below.

a) Maria does not like you leaving late at night.
b) You should sneak out without him noticing.
c) Taking part in a competition is more important than to win.
d) To lose is no disgrace.
e) I expect that not to know the answer does not surprise you.
f) To wash and to iron clothes take a lot of time.
g) To read helps me to relax.
h) To sunbath can be very dangerous at times.
i) I hope me arriving late does not inconvenience you.
j) Molema enjoys to read adventure stories.
k) I hate him working so late at night.
l) Prof. Kruger dislikes you talking so loudly in the corridors.

EXERCISE 2

Form gerunds from the following infinitives.

a) to begin
b) to write
c) to lie
d) to canoe
e) to manoeuvre
f) to compete
g) to fulfil
h) to believe
i) to receive
j) to escape

EXERCISE 3

Complete the following sentences by choosing an appropriate gerund from the following list:

coming, setting, smoking, being, kissing, gazing, taking, staring, losing, refuting, parking, digging, having

a) We were told of your___.
b) Do you mind my_____off these shoes?
c) Beverley goes there at the risk of_____killed.
d) Miyeni risks___her job.
e) The taxi will be long___.
f) Mogale enjoys___at passersby.
g) Mbewe has the duty of a good example.
h) Since the rebuke, Maja has abstained from_____.
i) _____ at the examination timetable will do you no good.
j) This youngster likes___his puppy.

Chapter 12

Homophones

Spelling is a nightmare to most learners of English. Misspellings may be attributed to homophony. Homophones are words that are pronounced alike but differ in meaning and spelling. For example, hale/hail, cite/site, gate/gait, gild/guild, lone/loan, maize/maze, pole/poll, mite/might, etc.

Learners of English should take note of the difference between <u>homophones</u> and <u>homonyms</u>. The latter refers to words that are spelt alike and pronounced alike, but differ in meaning. For example, boil (to cook)/boil (a sore).

Example 1
- Mogano Selaelo has been advised to drop her case for lack of <u>prove</u>. *(wrong)*
- Mogano Selaelo has been advised to drop her case for lack of <u>proof</u>. *(correct)*

<u>Prove</u> is a verb and <u>proof</u> is the corresponding noun.

Example 2
- The pupils are <u>quite</u> today because they are writing a test. *(wrong)*
- The pupils are <u>quiet</u> today because they are writing a test. *(correct)*

<u>Quite</u> is an adverb of degree. It is not the right word to use here. <u>Quiet</u> (i.e. not making a noise) is the right word. It is an <u>adjective</u>.

Example 3
- The estate agent has many new houses for <u>sell</u>. *(wrong)*
- The estate agent has many new houses for <u>sale</u>. *(correct)*

<u>Sale</u> and <u>sell</u> both relate to <u>selling</u>; but <u>sell</u> is a <u>verb</u>, while <u>sale</u> is a <u>noun</u>.

Example 4
- To guard against theft, you should leave all your valuables in a <u>save</u>. *(wrong)*

- To guard against theft, you should leave all your valuables in a <u>safe</u>. (*correct*)

<u>Save</u> is a <u>verb</u>, <u>safe</u> is a <u>noun</u> (i.e. a strong metal cupboard with special locks). Note that <u>safe</u> is also an adjective. For example, I don't feel <u>safe</u> in here.

Example 5

- Evelyn Makgokga was told to <u>park</u> her belongings and vacate the hotel room immediately. (*wrong*)
- Evelyn Makgokga was told to <u>pack</u> her belongings and vacate the hotel room immediately. (*correct*)

<u>Park</u> and <u>pack</u> have a similar sound and may confuse users of English. <u>Park</u> is generally used with vehicles, and means 'leave your vehicle somewhere temporarily.' <u>Pack</u> means 'gather things together.'

We would like to devote today's lesson to a study of some of those words that are frequently confused by students in their essays, letters and other forms of creative writing. Such confusion may stem from <u>homophony</u> (i.e. words pronounced in the same way but having different spellings and meanings) or <u>homonymy</u> (i.e. words spelt alike and pronounced alike, but differ in meaning).

SOMETIMES / SOMETIME

<u>Example</u>: I'll see you <u>sometimes</u> next week. This sentence is grammatically incorrect because the word <u>sometimes</u> indicates the frequency of an event or action. For example, I sometimes visit the museum on Sundays. On the other hand, <u>sometime</u> means <u>at a certain time</u>.

Say: I'll see you sometime next week.

STATIONERY / STATIONARY

<u>Example</u>: That police-van has been <u>stationery</u> for over three hours; there must be something wrong with it. This statement is ungrammatical. <u>Stationery</u> refers to paper, envelopes and other materials or equipment used for writing. Conversely, <u>stationary</u> means <u>not moving</u> or <u>immobile.</u>

Say: That police-van has been stationary for over three hours; there must be something wrong with it.

REMIND / REMEMBER

<u>Example</u>: Please <u>remember</u> me about my bag when I leave; I'm very forgetful these days. The above sentence is grammatically

unacceptable. Remember means bring something back to memory. On the contrary, to remind someone of something is to cause them not to forget it.

Say: Please remind me of my bag when I leave; I'm very forgetful these days.

TEMPORAL / TEMPORARY

Example: Peter has been employed on a temporal basis. The word temporal is not suitable in this context because it means relating to earthly rather than religious or spiritual things. On the other hand, temporary is the opposite of full-time or permanent.

Say: Peter has been employed on a temporary basis.

HEAT / HOT

Example: He took off his jacket because he was feeling too much heat. In good English, you don't feel heat; you feel hot. However, if the heat is specific (e.g. the tropical heat), it is acceptable to say you feel the heat. In this case, the use of the definite article is mandatory.

Say: He took off his jacket because he was feeling hot.

NATIONALISE / NATURALISE

Example: He emigrated to Canada and was nationalised Canadian. This sentence is incorrect because the verb nationalise is used when something becomes national property. If the government nationalises a private company or industry, that company or industry becomes state property and is controlled by the government. To naturalise means to acquire a citizenship; to become a citizen of a particular country.

Say: He emigrated to Canada and was naturalised Canadian.

In this lesson, I would like to dwell on frequent errors in written and spoken English that one may attribute to homophony. Look at the following pairs: loose /lose, affect /effect, adopt/adapt, already /all ready, toll/tall, altogether/all together.

Example 1
- This careless boy is always loosing his money. (*wrong*)
- This careless boy is always losing his money. (*correct*) Loose (= not firmly fixed) and lose (=misplace) are not synonyms.

Example 2
- Some of my students believe that alcohol abuse does not effect their academic output. (*wrong*)

- Some of my students believe that alcohol abuse does not affect their academic output. (*correct*)

Affect (=influence) and effect (=cause something to happen) are not synonymous verbs.

Example 3
- Innocent Munengwa adapted the Masarwa child. (*wrong*)
- Innocent Munengwa adopted the Masarwa child. (*correct*)

Adapt (=change something to make it suitable for a new purpose) and adopt (=take someone else's child into your own family) convey different meanings.

Example 4
- They had all ready voted for him at the first ballot. (*wrong*)
- They had already voted for him at the first ballot. (*correct*) All ready (=all prepared) and already (=at an earlier time) are different in meaning.

Example 5
- When Christian stopped visiting Vanessa all together, she found another boyfriend. (*wrong*)
- When Christian stopped visiting Vanessa altogether, she found another boyfriend. (*correct*)

All together (=all at the same time or place) and altogether (=completely) convey totally different meanings.

Example 6
- Drivers are required to pay an amount on tall roads as they move from one province to another. (*wrong*)
- Drivers are required to pay an amount at toll roads as they move from one province to another. (*correct*)

Tall (=having great height) and toll (=small amount of money) are not synonyms.

Some words which are near-homophones (words pronounced almost alike) are sometimes confused by users of English. This grammatical phenomenon is known as 'malapropism' (misapplication of words). In this lesson, we shall revisit some of the words that are a possible source of confusion to English second language speakers.

Example 1
- I think we should <u>adapt</u> Prof. Lenyai's sound suggestions. *(wrong)*
- I think we should <u>adopt</u> Prof. Lenyai' s sound suggestion. *(correct)*

Adopt =change something to make it look suitable for a new purpose or situation. Adapt =take someone else's idea, plan or way of behaving. The corresponding nouns are <u>adoption</u> (not adoptation) and <u>adaptation</u> (not adaption).

Example 2
- Please come and sit <u>besides</u> me. *(wrong)*
- Please, come and sit <u>beside</u> me. *(correct)*

Besides =in addition to / except, moreover. Beside =by the side of.

Example 3
- Moola played soccer <u>continually</u> for two weeks last summer. *(wrong)*
- Moola played soccer <u>continuously</u> for two weeks last summer. (correct)

Continually =always or frequently happening. Continuous =happening without interruption.

Example 4
- The candidates were <u>detracted</u> by the noise of passing cars. *(wrong)*
- The candidates were <u>distracted</u> by the noise of passing cars. *(correct)*

Detract from =take away from / depreciate. Distract =draw attention away from.

Example 5
- The GEAR policy has not promoted <u>economical</u> growth. *(wrong)*
- The GEAR policy has not promoted <u>economic</u> growth. *(correct)*

Economical =voiding unnecessary waste, for example, an economical way of carrying a project through = a way that saves the most money. Economic =having to do with the science of economics, for example, the economic policy of South Africa.

Malapropisms constitute a serious pitfall in English language communication. Speakers of English should guard against confusing the following pairs of words: insure/assure, distinct/distinctive, especially/specially, effective/efficacious, affect/effect.

EXERCISE 1
Use these homophones in sentences of your own to show that you understand the differences in meaning.

a) might/mite
b) pole/poll
c) pour/pore
d) rap/wrap
e) metal/mettle
f) gild/guild
g) fowl/foul
h) cymbal/symbol
i) hail/hale
j) maize/maze
k) wrung/rung
l) prize/pries
m) mowed/mode
n) hew/hue
o) isle/aisle
p) manner/manor
q) freeze/frieze
r) creak/creek
s) greater/grater

EXERCISE 2
Re-arrange the following words in pairs of homophones.

beau, course, paws, grate, coarse, bough, pores, great, wry, use, cession, sole, rye, soul, ewes, session, seize, quay, cease, key

Chapter 13

Idioms

Idiomatic (figurative) expressions play a significant role in communication, especially literature. We are all aware of the importance of imagery (metaphor, simile, hyperbole, euphemism, personification, etc.) in fictional writing. Imagery enlivens verse. It gives flavour and local colour to prose. The problem that arises is how to use these figures of speech in the proper way. A misplaced idiom is as good as no idiom at all.

Idioms are groups of words that have a different meaning when used together from the meaning they would convey when used individually. An idiom is a set expression that must be used exactly as it is. In other words, distortions in the morphology of an idiom alter its meaning or render it meaningless.

Example 1

- To me this sounds like wanting to <u>eat your cake and have it</u>. (*wrong*)
- To me this sounds like wanting to <u>have your cake and eat it</u>. (*correct*)

If you think that someone wants to have the benefits of doing two things when it is only reasonable to expect the benefits of doing one, you can say that they want to <u>have their cake and eat</u> it.

Example 2

- Jeremy has <u>a bonnet in his bee</u>, he insists the earth is not round but flat. (*wrong*)
- Jeremy has <u>a bee in his bonnet</u>, he insists the earth is not round but flat. (*correct*)

A bee in one's bonnet =an obsession; some particular idea or conviction, usually slightly crazy.

Example 3

- We gave the accused the <u>benefit of doubt</u>. (*wrong*)
- We gave the accused the <u>benefit of the doubt</u>. (*correct*) Give the benefit of the doubt =assume that a person is innocent when it is not certain that he is guilty.

Example 4
- I want to talk about our marriage but Anasthasia <u>keeps beating in the bush</u>. (*wrong*)
- I want to talk about our marriage but Anasthasia <u>keeps beating about the bush</u>. (*correct*)

Beat about the bush =avoid or delay a straightforward discussion; approach a subject in a roundabout way.

Example 5
- My father always reminds me that life nowadays is not <u>a bed of rose</u>. (*wrong*)
- My father always reminds me that life nowadays is not <u>a bed of roses</u>. (*correct*)

Bed of roses=a state of ease and luxury (frequently used within a negative expression).

In this lesson we shall take a look at some common mistakes in English that result from too close a translation into English of foreign idiomatic expressions. One must not lose sight of the fact that many English users are not native speakers of English. Consequently, there is often an unconscious translation of mother tongue expressions into English. A couple of examples would drive this point home.

Example 1
- We have to learn this poem <u>off head</u>. (*wrong*)
- We have to learn this poem <u>by heart</u>. (*correct*)

Notice that when you learn something by heart, you memorize it.

Example 2
- I <u>had</u> ten years when my father died. (*wrong*)
- I <u>was</u> ten years old when my father died. (*correct*) **OR**
- I <u>was aged</u> ten when my father died. (*correct*)

Example 3
- I am going to cut my hair at the barber's. (*wrong*)
- I am going to have my hair cut at the barber's. (*correct*) Notice that the implication of the first sentence is that you are going to the barber's shop to get his tools and do the hair-cutting yourself.

Example 4
- My watch works ten minutes behind. (*wrong*)

- My watch is ten minutes slow. (*correct*) English second language speakers also tend to say:
- My watch is ten minutes in front. (*wrong*)
- My watch is ten minutes fast. (*correct*)

Example 5
- I am inviting you to make a walk with me to the city. (*wrong*)
- I am inviting you to take a walk with me to the city. (*correct*)

OR
- I am inviting you to go for a walk with me to the city.

It should be noted that a walk is a journey that you make by walking, usually for pleasure.

Example 6
- The matrics have just done their examination. (*wrong*)
- The matrics have just taken their examination. (*correct*) **OR**
- The matrics have just sat (for) their examination. (*correct*)

OR
- The matrics have just written their examination. (*correct*)

It is noteworthy that a teacher gives or sets an examination; the students/pupils take or sit (for) the examination.

Example 7
- I saw a strange dream a fortnight ago. (*wrong*)
- I had a strange dream a fortnight ago. (*correct*) **OR**
- I dreamt (dreamed) a strange dream a fortnight ago. (*correct*)

Most English Second Language speakers tend to think in their mother tongues in the course of a conversation in English. This accounts for the worrisome linguistic interferences that have been discussed above. To minimize these errors, English Language speakers should endeavour to think and speak in English.

EXERCISE 1

Look up the meaning of each of the following idiomatic expressions below in a dictionary.

a) All that glitters in not gold.
b) He has a green eye.
c) To split hairs.
d) To live from hand to mouth.
e) Hard and fast rules.

f) To run with the hare and hunt with the hounds.
g) To have one's heart in one's mouth.
h) By hook or by crook.
i) At the eleventh hour.
j) In a jiffy.
k) Look before you leap.
l) The long and short of it.
m) Not up to the mark.
n) To put in a nutshell.
o) To pour oil on troubled waters.
p) To hold out the olive branch.
q) To pay the piper.
r) To pick to pieces.
s) To pin one's faith on.
t) To come to pass.

EXERCISE 2

Fill in the blanks below by choosing an appropriate idiom from the list.

If the cap fits wear it, on the brink, to bell the cat, to bide one's time, to draw a blank, to quarrel with one's bread and butter,
to rub up the wrong way.
a) Judas a won a prize but I_____.
b) A shrewd businessman will___before he acts.
e) I am sorry if that remark hurt you, but___.
d) When it comes to risks no one is prepared to_.
e) What are you going to get out of her if you continue to_?

Chapter 14

Infinitives Wrongly Used

In this lesson, I shall discuss some errors committed by speakers of English when they use the <u>infinitive</u> instead of the <u>gerund</u>. An infinitive is the <u>basic</u> form of a verb, for example, <u>do</u>, <u>be</u>, <u>take</u>, <u>eat</u>, etc. The infinitive is often used with 'to' in front of it. For example, <u>to do</u>, <u>to be</u>, <u>to take</u>, <u>to eat</u>, etc. A <u>gerund</u> is generally defined as a verbal noun. It is a noun formed from a verb which refers to an action, process or state. Gerunds end in '-ing,' for instance, <u>doing</u>, <u>being</u>, <u>taking</u>, <u>eating</u>, etc.

Example 1
- I look forward <u>to see</u> you at the party tonight. *(wrong)*
- I look forward to <u>seeing</u> you at the party tonight. *(correct)*

'Look forward to' means 'expect.' This expression should be followed by a <u>gerund</u> instead of an <u>infinitive</u> as seen above.

Example 2
- The minister said that there was no harm <u>to teach</u> sexuality in school. *(wrong)*
- The minister said that there was no harm <u>in teaching</u> sexuality in school. *(correct)*

The expression 'there is no harm doing' which means 'it might be worth doing' must be followed by a gerund, not an infinitive.

Example 3
- It is no good <u>to get angry</u> with everyone for no apparent reason. *(wrong)*
- It is no good <u>getting</u> angry with everyone for no apparent reason. *(correct)*

The expression 'no good' which means 'of no use' should be followed by a gerund as in the example above.

Example 4
- I am <u>tired to beg</u> students to do their assignments. *(wrong)*
- I am <u>tired of begging</u> students to do their assignments. *(correct)*

The gerund (not the infinitive) should be used after words that regularly take a preposition, such as <u>fond of</u>, <u>insist on</u>, <u>tired of</u>, <u>succeed in</u>, etc.

Example 5
- He enjoys <u>to play</u> soccer early in the morning. *(wrong)*
- He enjoys <u>playing</u> soccer early in the morning. *(correct)*

Example 6
- The principal <u>insisted to expel</u> the pupil who drank liquor on the school premises. *(wrong)*
- The principal <u>insisted on expelling</u> the pupil who drank liquor on the school premises. *(correct)*

Example 7
- The police <u>succeeded to arrest</u> the pupil who shot his teacher to death. *(wrong)*
- The police <u>succeeded in arresting</u> the pupil who shot his teacher to death. *(correct)*

Example 8
- June 16 is a date <u>worth to remember</u> in the history of this country. *(wrong)*
- June 16 is a date <u>worth remembering</u> in the history of this country. *(correct)*

If something is <u>worth remembering</u>, it is considered to be important enough to remember.

Example 9
- He takes great pleasure <u>to help</u> the poor. *(wrong)*
- He takes great pleasure <u>in helping</u> the poor. *(correct)* Someone who takes pleasure in doing something, finds that activity enjoyable or satisfactory.

Note: The misuse of gerunds and infinitives is a recurrent problem in the original writing component (paper 1) of most exams. English language teachers would do well to devote ample time to this aspect of the syllabus.

This lesson focuses on frequent errors in spoken and written English attributable to the incorrect use of the <u>infinitive</u> form of verbs. In quite a few cases, it is desirable to use the <u>present continuous</u> tense of the verbs in question. We shall use a couple of examples to illustrate the point.

Example 1
- He simply walked away instead of <u>to wait</u>. *(wrong)*
- He simply walked away instead of <u>waiting</u>. *(correct)* **OR**
- Instead of waiting he simply walked away.

It is advisable to use the present continuous tense after prepositions or prepositional phrases.

Example 2
- I can see that he is quite incapable <u>to do</u> that. *(wrong)*
- I can see that he is quite incapable of <u>doing</u> that. *(correct)*

Notice that the above construction is also desirable for words such as <u>capable</u>, <u>able</u> and <u>unable</u>, etc.

Example 3
- This woman enjoys <u>to dance</u>. *(wrong)*
- This woman enjoys <u>dancing</u>. *(correct)*

The expression 'to be fond of' would also take a verb in the present continuous tense. For example, <u>this woman is fond of dancing</u>.

Example 4
- These youngsters always think <u>to go</u> to America. *(wrong)*
- These youngsters always think of <u>going</u> to America. *(correct)*

Notice that 'dream of' would also take the present continuous tense. For example, <u>these youngsters always dream of going to America</u>.

Example 5
- Soldiers are <u>used to get</u> up early in the morning. *(wrong)*
- Soldiers are <u>used to getting</u> up early in the morning. *(correct)*

Notice that the expression 'accustomed to' would also take the present continuous tense. For instance, <u>soldiers are accustomed to getting up early in the morning</u>.

Example 6
- You cannot always avoid <u>to make</u> mistakes. *(wrong)*
- You cannot always avoid <u>making</u> mistakes. *(correct)*

The expression 'can't help' would equally take the present continuous tense. For instance, <u>you can't help making mistakes</u>.

Example 7
- Please excuse <u>me to be so</u> late. *(wrong)*
- Please excuse me for <u>being</u> so late. *(correct)*

It is also correct to say please excuse my being late.

In a previous lesson we pinpointed some errors that stem from the wrong use of the -ing participle. In this lesson, we would be looking at some mistakes that arise from the use of the infinitive instead of the -ing participle.

Example 1
- This baby is not used to eat three heavy meals a day. (*wrong*)
- This baby is not used to eating three heavy meals a day. (*correct*)

'Be used,' should not be mistaken for the auxiliary 'used to' which is generally followed by an infinitive.

Example 2
- My father doesn't appreciate you to visit us at odd hours of the night. (*wrong*)
- My father doesn't appreciate your visiting us at odd hours of the night. (*correct*)

Example 3
- My kid sister strongly objects to be sent to a boarding school. (*wrong*)
- My kid sister strongly objects to being sent to a boarding school. (*correct*)

Example 4
- Instead of to worry about his academic failure, Rabia should work harder. (*wrong*)
- Instead of worrying about his academic failure, Rabia should work harder. (*correct*)

Note that you may use 'rather than' as an alternative construction. For example, rather than worry about his academic failure, Rabia should work harder.

Example 5
- He is angry because instead of them to investigate the matter, they simply fired him. (*wrong*)
- He is angry because instead of investigating the matter, they simply fired him. (*correct*)

Once again, it is possible to use 'rather than' in the example above. For example, he is angry because rather than investigate the matter, they simply fired him.

Example 6
- Masekoameng is opposed to <u>be arrested</u> without a warrant. (*wrong*)
- Masekoameng is opposed <u>to being</u> arrested without a warrant. (*correct*)

This lesson focuses on some common mistakes in English owning to the incorrect use of the infinitive.

There are two types of infinitives. The one is called the 'to' infinitive. It consists of 'to' and the base form of a verb. For instance, <u>to go</u>, <u>to write</u>, <u>to bring</u>, etc. The other is called the 'infinitive without to' or the 'bare infinitive.' For instance, he helped me <u>get</u> settled here. All too often, speakers of English distort the syntax of English by inserting an adverb between the 'to' and the 'verb' in the infinitive.

Example 1
- They wanted to <u>really</u> go to the movie. (*wrong*).
- They <u>really</u> wanted to go to the movie. (*correct*)

By simply moving the adverb <u>really</u> to the initial position in the sentence, we are able to undo the ambiguity.

Example 2
- When she saw the plane she wished to <u>desperately</u> fly. (*wrong*)
- When she saw the plane she <u>desperately</u> wished to fly. (*correct*)

Example 3
- We wanted to <u>really</u> thank our sponsors for making the event a resounding success. (*wrong*)
- We <u>really</u> wanted to thank our sponsors for making the event a resounding success. (*correct*)

Example 4
- They had to walk to Spar to <u>quickly</u> buy some meat. (*wrong*)
- They had to <u>quickly</u> walk to Spar to buy some meat. (*correct*)

Example 5
- During Easter I want to <u>honestly</u> repent. (*wrong*)
- During Easter I <u>honestly</u> want to repent. (*correct*)

Users of English should take cognizance of the fact that splitting an infinitive often leads to wrong grammatical usage.

EXERCISE 1
Identify the infinitives in the following sentences.
a) To swim is pleasant in summer.

b) They decided to return to school.
c) My ambition is to become a teacher.
d) He was about to speak when I interrupted him.
e) Robert was determined to master the art of windsurfing.
f) "To be or not to be" that is the question.
g) I wanted to escape from here but he stopped me.
h) We asked Don to go to the cinema.
i) You have to listen to your parents.
j) He had the urge to blow up the aircraft.

EXERCISE 2

Some sentence constructions require either the infinitive or the bare infinitive (i.e. infinitive without 'to'). Correct the sentences below.

a) Don't let Jimmy to go all by himself.
b) She made me to write the sentence thrice in my workbook.
c) I couldn't help to laugh when she told me the story.
d) Johnny made her to feel unwanted.
e) I heard him opened the door at midnight.

Chapter 15

Lexical Errors

A great many errors made by speakers of English may be termed lexical errors. 'Lexical' means relating to the words of a language. In linguistics, the words of a language can be referred to as the 'lexis' of that language.

Example 1
- Susan Mashulo said she would like to make friendship with me. (*wrong*)
- Susan Mashulo said she would like to make friends with me. (*correct*) **OR**
- Susan Mashulo said she would like to be friends with me. (*correct*)

'To be friends with someone' is an idiomatic expression that means 'begin friendship' with someone.

Example 2
- Only a negligible amount of people attended the conference. (*wrong*)
- Only a negligible number of people attended the conference. (*correct*)

An amount of something is how much there is, or how much you have, need, etc. This word is generally used before uncountable nouns (i.e. nouns which refer to things such as substances, qualities, feelings, etc).

Example 3
- Hasina said it was because of her likeness for me that she invited me to her house. (*wrong*)
- Hasina said it was because of her liking for me that she invited me to her house. (*correct*) **OR**
- Hasina said it was because she liked me that she invited me to her house. (*correct*)

Likeness means 'resemblance' and should not be confused with 'liking' which means 'love' or 'affection.'

Example 4

- This boy is an <u>academician</u> studying at Capricorn High School. (*wrong*)
- This boy is a <u>pupil</u> (student) at Capricorn High School. (*correct*)

The word 'academician' is out of place in this context. An 'academician' is a member of an academy, usually one that has been formed to promote and maintain standards in a particular field of study.

Example 5
- Dhanya paid a heavy <u>prize</u> for her dishonesty. (*wrong*)
- Dhanya paid a heavy <u>price</u> for her dishonesty. (*correct*) 'Prize' and 'price' are often confused because of their similarity in pronunciation. 'Prize' means 'reward' and this is not the word required in sentence 1 above. The appropriate word is 'price' which means 'cost.'

Quite a few mistakes made by users of English are attributable to the wrong use of lexis (words). Fowler (1965) calls this phenomenon 'haziness' and defines it as follows: a writer's failure to make a clear distinction between the different components of a sentence or clause, with the result that they run into one another. He provides the following examples for clarity.

Example 1
- I should wonder if he <u>didn't fall</u>. (*hazy*)
- I should wonder if he <u>fell</u>. (*clear*)

It is incorrect to insert the negative <u>didn't</u> already implied in <u>shouldn't</u>.

Example 2
- It is a pity that an account of American activities in aircraft production cannot yet be described. (*hazy*)
- It is a pity that American activities in aircraft production cannot yet be described. (*clear*) **OR**
- It is a pity that an account of American activities in aircraft production cannot be given. (*clear*)

<u>Account</u> is contained in <u>described</u>. Consequently, it is necessary to omit <u>an account of</u> or change <u>described</u> to <u>given</u> as in sentence 2.

Example 3

- Hitherto, the only way of tackling the evil was by means of prohibiting exportation from certain places. (*hazy*)
- Hitherto, the only way of tackling the evil was by prohibiting exportation from certain places. (*clear*)

Way and means overlap in sentence 1.

Example 4
- The welfare of the poor and needy was a duty that devolved especially on those who had a seat in the House. (*hazy*)
- Securing the welfare of the poor and needy was a duty that devolved especially on those who had a seat in the House. (*clear*)

It is not the welfare, but the securing of it that is a duty on those who had a seat in the House.

Example 5
- The need for some effort, a joint effort if possible, is an urgent necessity for all the interests concerned. (*hazy*)
- The need for some effort, a joint effort if possible, is urgent for all the interests concerned. (*clear*)

Need and necessity overlap in sentence 1.

The aim of this lesson is to pinpoint some lexical differences between American and British English. In this lesson we are concerned with American words other than slang. The following differences are noteworthy:

BRITISH	AMERICAN	
tin	can	
dustbin	garbage can	
boot (of a car)	trunk	
pavement	sidewalk	
petrol	gas (gasoline)	
lift	elevator	
braces	suspenders	
vest	undershirt	
waistcoat	vest	
chemist	druggist	
note (paper money)	bill	
BRITISH	**AMERICAN**	
bill (in a restaurant)	check shop	store
timber	lumber	
cupboard	closet	

biscuits	crackers
corngrain	
maize	corn
sweets	candies
presently	soon
draughts	checkers
tap	faucet
pack (of cards)	deck
government school	public school
public school	private school

Example 1
- I'll be meeting her at home <u>presently</u>. (*BrE*)
- I'll be meeting her at home <u>soon</u>. (*AmE*)

Example 2
- My wife bought some <u>sweets</u> for our kids. (*BrE*)
- My wife bought some <u>candies</u> for our kids. (*AmE*)

Example 3
- He opened the <u>boot</u> of his car to put my luggage in. (*BrE*)
- He opened the <u>trunk</u> of his car to put my luggage in. (*AmE*)

Example 4
- A haggard-looking man lay on the <u>pavement</u>. (*BrE*)
- A haggard-looking man lay on the <u>sidewalk</u>. (*AmE*)

Example 5
- The right thing to do with insulting letters is to throw them into the <u>dustbin. (*BrE*)</u>
- The right thing to do with insulting letters is to throw them into the <u>garbage can</u>. (*AmE*)

A sizeable number of errors committed by speakers of English are attributable to a limited vocabulary. In order to help you enrich your vocabulary, we would like you to do the following exercises.

EXERCISE 1

Supply one word for the following explanations.

a) A book in which the events of each day are recorded

_____

b) A book containing information on all branches of knowledge

_____

c) An extract or selection from a book

d) Language which is confusing and unintelligible

e) A declaration of the plans and promises put forward by a candidate for election, political party or sovereign

f) An error in printing or misprint _____
g) The exclusive right of an author or his/her heirs to publish or sell copies of his/her writings _____
h) Passing off another author's work as one's own

i) A record of one's life written by oneself _____
j) The history of the life of a person _____

EXERCISE 2
Supply a single word for each of the phrases relating to science and the arts.
a) The study of birds _____
b) The study of stars _____
c) The natural history of animals _____
d) The study of ancient buildings and prehistoric remains

e) The art of cultivating and managing gardens _____
f) The study of rocks and soils _____
g) The study of humankind _____
h) The science of colours _____
i) The scientific study of industrial arts _____
j) The science of the structure of the human body _____

Chapter 16

Malapropisms

The recurrence of malapropisms (words commonly confused) in English language communication has spurred me to write this lesson. The term 'malapropism' is generally associated with a certain Mrs. Malaprop, who tended to use the right word in the wrong place. This error is repeatedly committed by non-native speakers of English. We shall use a couple of examples to put users of English on their guard.

Example 1
- This shirt is expensive, I can't <u>effort</u> it. (*wrong*)
- This shirt is expensive, I can't <u>afford</u> it. (*right*)

Example 2
- The <u>affect</u> of drugs on the brain is <u>quiet</u> damaging. (*wrong*)
- The <u>effect</u> of drugs on the brain is <u>quite</u> damaging. (*correct*)

Example 3
- <u>Must</u> street kids <u>leave</u> on food picked from rubbish bins. (*wrong*)
- <u>Most</u> street kids <u>live</u> on food picked from rubbish bins. (*correct*)

Example 4
- You must <u>live</u> no stone unturned as you prepare for your <u>feature</u>. (*wrong*)
- You must <u>leave</u> no stone unturned as you prepare for your <u>future</u>. (*correct*)

Example 5
- We have to <u>rise</u> some <u>funs</u> for our social function. (*wrong*)
- We have to <u>raise</u> some <u>funds</u> for our social function. (*correct*)

Example 6
- You <u>most no</u> that laziness is the <u>course</u> of failure in <u>must</u> schools. (*wrong*)
- You <u>must know</u> that laziness is the <u>cause</u> of failure in <u>most</u> schools. (*correct*)

Example 7

- The <u>hole</u> class went to the exhibition <u>accept</u> me. (*wrong*)
- The <u>whole</u> class went to the exhibition <u>except</u> me. (*correct*)

Example 8
- I <u>fill</u> very happy because I've found the <u>write</u> answer. (*wrong*)
- I <u>feel</u> very happy because I've found the <u>right</u> answer. (*correct*)

Example 9
- I should <u>remember</u> you that you are <u>waisting</u> your time in school. (*wrong*)
- I should <u>remind</u> you that you are <u>wasting</u> your time in school. (*correct*)

Example 10
- I feel very <u>said</u> because <u>their</u> are no jobs in this country. (*wrong*)
- I feel very <u>sad</u> because <u>there</u> are no jobs in this country. (*correct*)

Example 11
- Our School is headed by a <u>temporal principle</u>. (*wrong*)
- Our School is headed by a <u>temporary principal</u>. (*correct*)

Example 12
- I <u>thing</u> we should <u>advertise</u> this big <u>full</u>. (*wrong*)
- I <u>think</u> we should <u>advise</u> this big <u>fool</u>. (*correct*)

EXERCISE 1

Malapropisms are sometimes called 'howlers' (stupid mistakes). Read the sentences below, identify the howlers and correct them.

a) The dog leapt out of its kernel and bit the passerby.
b) A plagiarist is a writer of plays.
c) An epitaph is a short sarcastic saying or poem.
d) Predestination is the thief of time.
e) Eve was tempted by a servant in the Garden of Eden.
f) All the students are certified with their marks.
g) An octopus is a person who is between eighty and eighty-nine years old.
h) A cyber is a secret system of writing that you can use to send messages.

i) Quadrupeds are four children born to the same mother at the same time.

j) Spaghetti is thrown on people at weddings.

EXERCISE 2

Correct the malapropisms in the sentences below.

a) The dinosaur is a large reptile that is <u>extant</u> now.

b) The act of marrying many wives is called <u>bigamy</u>.

c) <u>Unaware</u> means the clothes that we wear under our clothes.

d) Some people were put to death by <u>elocution</u>.

e) An admiral is a senior officer who commands a <u>navel</u> or fleet of ships.

f) The doctor felt the patient's <u>purse</u>.

g) A <u>corps</u> is a dead person.

h) I cannot read your handwriting; it is <u>eligible</u>.

i) Doctors generally use <u>cynical</u> thermometers.

j) Louis XIV of France was <u>gelatined</u>.

Chapter 17

Misrelated Participles

In this lesson we shall examine some communication problems in English that may be attributed to 'misrelated participles.'

Participles are used in forming tenses in English.

The present participle always ends in -ing for example, seeing the chimpanzee, the visitors joined the group of spectators.

The past participle, on the other hand, normally ends in -en, -ed, -d, or t. Problems generally crop up when speakers fail to relate the participle to the noun it describes as seen in the following examples.

Example 1
- Running to get away, the police caught the thief. (*wrong*)
- The police caught the thief as he was running away. (*correct*)

OR

- The police caught the thief when he was trying to run away. (*correct*)

Example 2
- Smiling at the baby, a rock made the old woman trip. (*wrong*)
- A rock made the old woman trip when she was smiling at the baby. (*correct*)

Example 3
- Playing outside, a storm caught the kids. (*wrong*)
- A storm caught the kids as they were playing outside. (*correct*)

OR

- A storm caught the kids as they played outside. (*correct*) **OR**
- A storm caught the kids when they were playing outside. (*correct*)

Example 4
- Leaping over the last hurdle, the race was won. (*wrong*)
- The race was won after he had leapt over the last hurdle. (*correct*) **OR**

- After having <u>leapt</u> over the last hurdle he won the race. (*correct*)

Example 5
- <u>Walking</u> through the thicket, it began to rain. (*wrong*)
- It began to rain when we/he/she they <u>walked</u> through the thicket. (*correct*) **OR**
- As we/he/she they <u>walked</u> through the thicket, it began to rain. (*correct*)

The correction of errors stemming from misrelated participles sometimes calls for the insertion of nominative pronouns as seen in example 5 above.

In this lesson, we shall dwell on the problem of inaccurate expression of thought stemming from misplaced words. In English, when words such as <u>never</u>, <u>seldom</u>, <u>rarely</u>, <u>everybody</u>, <u>neither</u>, <u>nor</u>, <u>not</u>, <u>only</u> and <u>no sooner</u> are placed at the beginning of a complete clause, the verb must come before the subject as in a question. The following examples would illustrate the point.

Example 1
- <u>Never</u> I have heard such a thing in my life. (*wrong*)
- <u>Never</u> have I heard such a thing in my life. (*correct*)

Example 2
- <u>All</u> students are not hardworking. (*wrong*)
- Not <u>all</u> students are hardworking. (*correct*)

Note that the first sentence is wrong because it makes <u>all</u> students lazy.

Example 3
- <u>Everybody</u> does not like liquor. (*wrong*)
- Not <u>everybody</u> likes liquor. (*correct*)

Notice that the first sentence is incorrect because it makes everybody a teetotaler.

Example 4
- <u>Seldom</u> it rains in the desert. (*wrong*)
- It <u>seldom</u> rains in the desert. (*correct*)

Example 5
- <u>Rarely</u> he travels by air. (*wrong*)
- He <u>rarely</u> travels by air. (*correct*)

Note that seldom and rarely are not placed at the beginning of the clauses in examples 4 and 5 above because there is no subject-verb inversion.

Example 6
- Sipho neither speaks Afrikaans nor English. (*wrong*)
- Sipho speaks neither Afrikaans nor English. (*correct*)

The first sentence is wrong because correlative conjunctions (i.e. conjunctions used in pairs, like neither - nor, not only - but also, etc.) are normally placed before words of the same part of speech.

Example 7
- I only met her once after their marriage. (*wrong*)
- I met her only once after their marriage. (*correct*)

Notice that only is usually placed immediately before the word it qualifies. In the sentence above, only qualifies the adverb once and not the verb met.

Example 8
- I should have not gone. (*wrong*)
- I should not have gone. (*correct*)

In a sentence comprising the word not and a compound verb, it's desirable to put not immediately after the auxiliary.

Many errors made by speakers of English are associated with the wrong choice of word pattern. The use of -ing participle is a case in point.

Example 1
- Mr. Vania was about entering his house when thieves shot him dead. (*wrong*)
- Mr. Vania was about to enter his house when thieves shot dead. (*correct*)

Note, however, that if you choose to use 'on the point of' entering would be the correct word to use. Example: Mr. Vania was on the point of entering his house when thieves shot him dead.

Example 2
- Herouzer decided buying a new car to replace her old one. (*wrong*)
- Herouzer decided to buy a new car to replace her old one. (*correct*) **OR**

- Herouzer decided <u>on buying</u> a new car to replace her old one. (*correct*)

'Decided' is generally followed by an <u>infinitive</u> as seen in sentence 2 above. Conversely, 'decided on' would take a present participle <u>buying</u> as seen in sentence 3.

Example 3
- Children from formerly disadvantaged communities now desire <u>entering</u> higher institutions of learning. (*wrong*)
- Children from formerly disadvantaged communities now desire <u>to enter</u> higher institutions of learning. (*correct*)

As a verb, <u>desire</u> is generally followed by an <u>infinitive</u> (i.e. to + verb) as seen in sentence 2 above. As a noun, <u>desire</u> may be followed by a preposition (to/for). Example: He has a strong desire to help and care for people.

Example 4
- The court has refused <u>granting</u> him bail. (*wrong*)
- The court has refused to <u>grant</u> him bail. (*correct*)

Note that refuse may be followed by a noun. Example: The poor man has refused every <u>offer</u> of help.

Example 5
- This immigrant doesn't know <u>speaking</u> Sepedi. (*wrong*)
- This immigrant doesn't know how <u>to speak</u> Sepedi. (*correct*)

To 'know' how to do something is always followed by 'to.' Contrarily, you have to omit 'to' if it means 'know' someone. Example: Mary <u>knows</u> Jonas intimately.

EXERCISE 1
Give the correct form of the verb in brackets.

a) (Lean) forward and (kick) the horse, the rider raced at top speed.

b) Thirsty and (exhaust), the travelers who had (lose) their way in the forest (move) on.

c) The parrot kept on (screech) and (crane) its neck.

d) We had hardly (take) a step when the hyena (start) to howl.

e) I could have (swear) I had (see) nothing.

f) There was nothing to break the silence of the night except the (beat) of our hearts.

g) Even the police-dog has little chance of (find) the wounded animal.
h) The lady was all (excite) and (shake) like a leaf.
i) By the time the flames (die) out I had (fall) asleep.
j) The animal must have (sense) danger.

EXERCISE 2
Fill the blanks by forming a participle from the verb in brackets.
a) _____ two wives is unacceptable in some churches. (marry)
b) Lingering is another word for_about. (hang)
c) In some buses_is not allowed. (smoke)
d) _____ is a synonym for petting. (pamper)
e) An____is a ticklish feeling. (itch)
f) _____ animals bring back food from their stomach into their mouth and chew it again. (ruminate)
g) Baba was away when the crime was___. (commit)
h) A dog leapt out of its kennel and_____furiously at the stranger. (bark)
i) Genetically___food is not good for our health. (modify)
j) All the teachers are___with the pupils' performance. (satisfy)

Chapter 18

Misspellings

In this lesson I will be shedding some light on recurrent spelling errors that I have picked up in the classwork of my pupils and from exam scripts that I have marked. A 'misspelling' is a word that has been spelt wrongly. There is ample evidence pointing to the fact that many speakers of English misspell words because they cannot pronounce them correctly. In most cases this inability stems from the influence of the speaker's mother tongue (native language) on the English language.

Example 1
- I am totally <u>dissapointed</u> to see the degree of indiscipline that reigns in SA schools these days. (*wrong*)
- I am totally <u>disappointed</u> to see the degree of indiscipline that reigns in SA schools these days. (*correct*)

Example 2
- For a long time I couldn't <u>dicide</u> whether the students were insane or just stupid. (*wrong*)
- For a long time I couldn't <u>decide</u> whether the students were insane or just stupid. (*correct*)

Example 3
- Child psychologists <u>belive</u> that a well-groomed child is an <u>obidient</u> person. (*wrong*)
- Child psychologists <u>believe</u> that a well-groomed child is an <u>obedient</u> person. (*correct*)

Example 4
- Tondani's mother <u>dissaproved</u> of her wearing revealing clothes to school. (*wrong*)
- Tondani's mother <u>disapproved</u> of her wearing revealing clothes to school. (*correct*)

Example 5
- Most youngsters <u>belive</u> in satanism and black magic <u>now our days</u>. (*wrong*)

- Most youngsters <u>believe</u> in satanism and black magic <u>nowadays</u>. (*correct*)

Example 6

- My eldest daughter shall be <u>recieving</u> her first Holy Communion next Sunday. (*wrong*)
- My eldest daughter shall be <u>receiving</u> her first Holy Communion next Sunday. (*correct*)

Example 7

- Alcoholics are notorious for <u>there</u> ability to <u>decieve</u> themselves about the extent of their problem. (*wrong*)
- Alcoholics are notorious for <u>their</u> ability to deceive themselves about the extent of their problem. (*correct*)

Constant reference to the dictionary is a good remedy for misspelling problems.

The aim of this lesson is to enable learners to establish a clear distinction between Americanisms (American English) and British English. It is common knowledge that American English is penetrating British English at a terrific pace through the mass media and other channels of communication. We are concerned here with spellings. Not all American spellings are unacceptable. Spellings such as: <u>color</u>, <u>defense</u>, <u>judgment</u>, <u>mold</u>, <u>anesthetic</u>, <u>jewelery</u>, <u>honor</u>, <u>labor</u>, <u>flavor</u> and <u>more</u> are as good as their British equivalents but are usually considered incorrect by examiners, editors and other language practitioners working outside the United States of America and Canada. Our word of caution is: when in Rome do as the Romans do, which means avoid Americanisms until you settle in the United States.

Example 1

- <u>Labor</u> Day is a public holiday in <u>honor</u> of working people all over the world. (*AmE*)
- <u>Labour</u> Day is a public holiday in <u>honour</u> of working people all over the world. (*BrE*)

Example 2

- Local <u>color</u> adds <u>flavor</u> to fictional writing. (*AmE*)
- Local <u>colour</u> adds <u>flavour</u> to fictional writing. (*BrE*)

Example 3

- He insisted on conducting his own <u>defense</u>. (*AmE*)

- He insisted on conducting his own <u>defence</u>. (*BrE*)

Example 4
- Nuclear proliferation has returned to <u>center</u> stage in international affairs. (*AmE*)
- Nuclear proliferation has returned to <u>centre</u> stage in international affairs. (*BrE*)

Example 5
- She has become so fond of me, almost against her better <u>judgment</u>. (*AmE*)
- She has become so fond of me, almost against her better <u>judgement</u>. (*BrE*)

Example 6
- Too often we try to <u>mold</u> our children into something they do not wish to be. (*AmE*)
- Too often, we try to <u>mould</u> our children into something they do not wish to be. (*BrE*)

EXERCISE 1

Correct the spelling errors in the sentences below.

a) Sivil servants will recieve the news with great joy.
b) The male will be replased by the female.
c) What you have done is not klear at all.
d) A computer kan do multiplikasion.
e) I took a niece fotograf of that building yesterday.
f) The publik is hereby informed that the library will be klosed from 14h -16h tomorrow.
g) I want to built a hause for myself next year.
h) Your English language aksent is not akurate.
i) This horible behaviour is very disgrasful.
j) This is quite a komplicated problem.

EXERCISE 2

There are misspelt words in the sentences below. Identify and correct them.

a) This is the dawn of the new millenium.
b) Nhlapo has all ready booked for his accomodation.
c) We are trying to intergrate enviromental education into the new curicullum.

d) Cliff Olivier has stressed the importance of enviromental heath.

e) Derick du Toit can do a lot of things, for instence, drive, cook and dence.

f) We are totaly comitted to this cause.

g) Muller stands to benefitt from this project.

h) Pat Venter didn't have a bathe for the hole week.

i) Phuti has made an error of omision.

j) Ladies and gentlemen, you are all very well come to this occasion.

EXERCISE 3

Rewrite the following paragraph, correcting all wrongly spelt words.

Every sekond of every day babys are born all over the world. This means that mor people are dipending on the earth and its netural resorces to provid them with what they need to surviv. It is therefor importent for us all and fatur generations to learn to apreciate these resorces. We are a throw-away nasion, our plannet is becoming a huge dumb.

Chapter 19

Modifiers

The focus of this lesson is the use of <u>modifiers</u> in communication. Modifiers refer to words, phrases or clauses which modify the meaning of other words in a sentence. In order to avoid incomprehension, a modifier should be placed as closely as possible to the word it relates to. The contrary would lead to ambiguity. Adverbial and adjectival phrases need to be placed carefully for fear of distorting intended meaning in communication.

Example 1
- A new computer is now on sale in shops called pentium. (*wrong*)
- A new computer called pentium is now on sale in shops. (*correct*)

Sentence 1 would be correct (acceptable) if there is a chain of shops called <u>pentium</u> but the intended meaning is that provided in sentence 2. Generally, problems of this nature arise when modifiers are placed at the end of sentences without adequate reflection on where they really belong.

Example 2
- As a taxpayer, the embezzlement of public funds concerns me. (*wrong*)
- As a taxpayer, I am concerned about the embezzlement of public funds. (*correct*)

After the adjectival modifier 'as a taxpayer' the reader expects a noun/pronoun to which the modifier refers.

Example 3
- You should stop eating fatty foods to lose weight. (*wrong*)
- To lose weight, you should stop eating fatty foods. (*correct*)

The placing of 'to lose weight' next to fatty foods, implies that 'fatty foods' are being eaten by you in order to lose weight. It is self evident that communicators have to handle infinitives with extreme care as seen above.

Example 4
- Starting from the campus, the railway station can be reached in a few minutes. (*wrong*)
- If you start from the campus the railway station can be reached in a few minutes. (*correct*) **OR**
- Starting from the campus you/people/visitors, etc. can reach the railway station in a few minutes.

In this lesson we shall focus attention on some communication problems that stem from the incorrect positioning of modifying participles. The general rule in grammar is that when there are more than one noun/pronoun in a sentence, the modifying participle should be attached to the nearest noun/pronoun in the sentence.

Example 1
- While running to school, rain forced Thabang to take shelter. (*wrong*)
- While he was running to school, rain forced Thabang to take shelter. (*correct*)

Grammatically, rain is running to school in sentence 1 above. Either the appropriate word should be placed next to the modifier as seen in sentence 2 or the non-finite participle 'running' should be made finite, so that there is no ambiguity about who is performing the action of 'running.'

Example 2
- Referring to your correspondence of June 28, the goods have now been delivered. (*ambiguous*)
- I refer to your correspondence of June 28. The goods have now been delivered. (*clear*) **OR**
- Referring to your correspondence of June 28, I am glad to say that the goods have now been delivered.

In sentence 1, the modifying participle 'referring' attaches itself to the nearest noun 'goods' as though the goods were doing the action of 'referring.' This has been corrected in sentence 2 by changing the non-finite modifier into a finite statement. In sentence 3, we have inserted an appropriate pronoun 'I' to take off the ambiguity.

Example 3
- Not knowing the town well, it is difficult for me to guide you. (*ambiguous*)

- As I don't know the town well, I have difficulty guiding you. (*clear*) **OR**
- Not knowing the town well, I have difficulty guiding you. (*clear*)

In sentence 1, the modifier attaches itself to 'it' in a rather meaningless way.

Example 4
- Considering his position, my father decided to resign. (*ambiguous*)
- After considering his position, my father decided to resign. (*clear*)

The following lesson dwells on some common errors in written and spoken English stemming from dangling modifiers. A dangling modifier is a word that is unintentionally linked to another word in a sentence.

Dangling modifiers are also called isolated, unrelated or suspended modifiers. The effect produced by such modifiers is often comical. Sometimes it results in ambiguity. We shall use practical examples to illustrate this point.

Example 1
- <u>Running</u> across the street, a taxi hit the pupil. (*wrong*)
- A taxi hit the pupil as he ran across the street. (*correct*) **OR**
- A taxi hit the pupil while he was running across the street. (*correct*)

Grammatically, the first sentence is wrong because it gives the impression that the taxi was running across the street, and not the pupil.

Example 2
- Returning from work late at night, thieves robbed Thomas at gunpoint. (*wrong*)
- Thieves robbed Thomas at gunpoint when he was returning from work late at night. (*correct*) **OR**
- Thieves robbed Thomas at gunpoint as he was returning from work late at night. (*correct*)

The modifier 'returning' is mistakenly attached to thieves whereas it was Thomas who was returning.

Example 3
- By attending classes, the teacher wouldn't teach me anything new. (*wrong*)
- The teacher wouldn't teach me anything new if I attend classes. (*correct*) **OR**
- By attending classes, I wouldn't learn anything new from the teacher. (*correct*)

The modifier 'attending' has been wrongly linked to 'teacher' instead of 'I.' This makes the first sentence ambiguous (unclear).

Example 4
- Born to a poor family, I couldn't understand how he managed to lead a life of luxury. (*wrong*)
- I couldn't understand how he managed to lead a life of luxury given that he was born to a poor family. (*correct*)

Example 5
- While waiting for you outside the shed, rain started pouring down and I got completely drenched. (*wrong*)
- As I waited for you outside the shed, rain started pouring down and I got completely drenched. (*correct*)

The first sentence is incorrect because the speaker has mistakenly attached the modifying word 'waiting' to rain. It is 'I' (speaker) that was waiting, and not the 'rain.'

Notice that the correction of errors stemming from the misuse of dangling modifiers sometimes calls for a complete restructuring of the sentence as seen in the examples above.

It is also noteworthy that some modifiers are idiomatic and therefore require careful usage. These include expressions such as referring to, owing to, judging by, granting, etc. English language speakers would do well to handle these expressions with extra care.

This lesson aims at shedding some light on the use of single word modifiers, namely only, even, almost, often and unlike. Generally, errors result from the improper use of the aforementioned words. A couple of examples would illustrate the point.

Example 1
- I only saw Lorraine yesterday. (i.e. I didn't talk or do anything else to her)

- I saw Lorraine <u>only</u> yesterday. (i.e. I saw her as recently as yesterday)

The positioning of the word <u>only</u> does often make much difference in terms of meaning. There are times when careless positioning may lead to ambiguity.

- We may <u>only</u> unlock the chess. (i.e. and do nothing else)
- <u>Only</u> we can unlock the chess. (and no-one else)
- We may unlock <u>only</u> the chess. (and nothing else that needs unlocking)

Example 2
- <u>Even</u> Thabo could not find the key. (let alone anyone else)
- Thabo could not <u>even</u> find the key. (let alone do anything with it)
- Thabo could not find <u>even</u> the key. (let alone any other thing)

<u>Even</u> should be placed in front of the word(s) to be emphasised or contrasted.

Example 3
- Mariam <u>almost</u> passed without noticing her mother. (but she didn't pass)
- Mariam passed <u>almost</u> without noticing her mother. (she did pass)

Example 4
- Players who injure themselves <u>often</u> have to pay higher insurance premiums. (*ambiguous*)
- Players who <u>often</u> injure themselves have to pay higher insurance premiums. (*clear*)
- Players who injure themselves <u>often</u> have to pay higher insurance premiums. (*clear*)

Example 5
- Unlike mom, dad enjoys reading detective novels. (*clear*)
- Unlike Nigeria and Ghana, central control of sports does not exist in South Africa. (*ambiguous*)

In Sentence 2, Nigeria and Ghana are contrasted with central control whereas the intended contrast is between Nigeria and Ghana, and South Africa.

EXERCISE 1

Rewrite these sentences, putting the modifiers in the appropriate positions.

a) Strolling in the street were a group of well-dressed youngsters.

b) Considering all circumstances, Mr. Smit has kept remarkably cheerful.

c) Following a police raid, Bentley was arrested.

d) The tanks on the battlefield that had been exploded prevented the advance of soldiers.

e) Although unreliable, Sebueng depends on the bus service.

f) Some countries have exceptionally high mountains, such as Kenya.

g) Preparation for the conference required not only hard work by men but also women.

h) The election resulted not only in the death of apartheid but also the birth of democracy in South Africa could be traced to the election.

i) Delport said he would either call the next day or the day after.

j) Etienne has neither phoned nor has he written.

EXERCISE 2

The wrong use of modifiers may lead to ambiguity. Rewrite the following sentences correctly.

a) Willis can speak very well German.

b) Caria likes very much exotic music.

c) As a beginner, Jan cannot speak perfectly French.

d) Deon explained very clearly the maths problem.

e) Richard shot with a gun a lion last week.

f) Caiphus put into his pocket the money.

g) Notshaya dislikes very much red wine.

h) Mgidlana learned by heart the poems.

i) Vald received from his uncle a Christmas gift.

j) Norman shut quickly the door of his shack.

Chapter 20

Negation

In this lesson, I would like to discuss some blunders committed by speakers of English as a result of the mishandling of negatives. Generally speaking, English grammarians regard two negatives as cancelling each other and producing an affirmative. For example, the proper meaning of 'nobody didn't laugh' is that 'everyone laughed.' The following examples should put English speakers on their guard.

Example 1
- This pupil is very dull, he <u>does not</u> know <u>nothing</u>. (*wrong*)
- This pupil is very dull, he knows nothing. (*correct*) **OR**
- This pupil is very dull, he does not know anything. (*correct*)

Example 2
- <u>No one didn't</u> go to the movie last night. (*wrong*)
- No one went to the movie last night. (*correct*) Notice that the implication of the first sentence is that everybody (everyone) went to the movie last night.

Example 3
- The policemen <u>couldn't</u> find <u>nothing</u> after searching the entire house. (*wrong*)
- The policemen couldn't find anything after searching the entire house. (*correct*) **OR**
- The policemen found nothing after searching the entire house. (*correct*)

The use of the two negatives <u>couldn't</u> and <u>nothing</u> in the first sentence renders it positive: The policemen found something after searching the entire house.

Example 4
- I <u>didn't</u> find him <u>nowhere</u>. (*wrong*)
- I didn't find him anywhere. (*correct*) **OR**
- I found him nowhere. (*correct*)

The double negation in the first sentence makes it affirmative: I found him somewhere.

Example 5
- We <u>didn't</u> learn <u>nothing</u> at school today. (*wrong*)
- We didn't learn anything at school today. (*correct*) **OR**
- We learnt (learned) nothing at school today. (*correct*)

Example 6
- These street kids <u>don't</u> respect <u>no one</u>. (*wrong*)
- These street kids respect no one. (*correct*) **OR**
- These street kids don't respect anyone. (*correct*)

The presence of two negatives <u>don't</u> and <u>no one</u> in the first sentence makes it positive. Consequently, the proper meaning of that sentence would be: These street kids respect everyone.

In some languages, for instance Greek, double negation is used intentionally for purposes of emphasis. In that case, one negative reinforces the other. The English used to do the same in vulgar speech. However, in contemporary educated English, it is desirable to avoid the use of double negation because, more often than not, it produces a meaning different from that intended by the speaker.

EXERCISE 1

Rewrite the following sentences in the <u>negative form</u>.

a) Molema went home yesterday.
b) Papo told us to wait there.
c) Maishamaite made a mistake during the mid-year exam.
d) Pieter broke the window deliberately.
e) Betty did the assignment in a desultory manner.
f) Babe speaks Zulu very fluently.
g) Emmerencia bought a new hat at Spar.
h) Mark found his missing book.
i) Terence arrived late from home.
j) Kennedy knows the answer.

EXERCISE 2

Answer the following questions in the negative.

a) Did your father buy a BMW?
b) Does your younger brother know how to swim?
c) Is it true that she didn't find her shoes?
d) Was it the prefect who rang the bell?
e) Did the professor teach anything new?

f) Is it true that the president flew to New York last week?
g) Did they solve the problem for you?
h) Does your mother speak many languages?
i) It looks like rain, isn't it?
j) Did the cops arrest the thief?

EXERCISE 3
Rewrite the following sentences correctly.
a) Lynne could not find Harry nowhere.
b) There isn't no one who knows the whereabouts of Epie.
c) Bill didn't see nobody in the hall.
d) Mbongeni did not tell me nothing.
e) Mondlane is not neither wise nor foolish.
f) Stephen will not find the money nowhere.
g) We did not give Trodger nothing.
h) Thebe doesn't know nothing in mathematics.
i) Charmaine did not speak to no one in the crowd.
j) Nobody never saw him with Belinda.

Chapter 21

Number

In this lesson, I will be discussing errors in written English that stem from wrong pluralization of nouns. <u>Number</u> in English refers to the <u>singular</u> and <u>plural</u> forms of nouns. A <u>countable</u> noun has both singular and plural forms (e.g. car - cars, orange - oranges, book - books, etc). Some nouns take <u>s</u> in the plural form as seen above. Others take <u>es</u> (e.g. box - <u>boxes</u>). Some others need some internal substitution in order to derive the plural form (e.g. wife - wives, leaf - leaves, etc).

Example 1
- Traditional Africans have several religious <u>believes</u>. (*wrong*)
- Traditional Africans have several religious <u>beliefs</u>. (*correct*)

<u>Belief</u> (=your views on religion and other matters) is an exception in English. Its plural form is derived by simply adding an <u>s</u>.

Example 2
- Most traditional leaders tend to marry many <u>wifes</u> when they are enthroned. (*wrong*)
- Most traditional leaders tend to marry many <u>wives</u> when they are enthroned. (*correct*)

The plural form of the noun <u>wife</u> is derived by substituting <u>v</u> for <u>f</u> before affixing an <u>s</u>.

Example 3
- The police at Seshego arrested one hundred and fifty <u>thiefs</u> last night. (*wrong*)
- The police at Seshego arrested one hundred and fifty <u>thieves</u> last night. (*correct*)

You have to substitute <u>v</u> for <u>f</u> followed by an <u>e</u> in order to obtain the plural form <u>thieves</u>.

Example 4
- The radio and television provide the general public with a lot of <u>informations</u>. (*wrong*)
- The radio and television provide the general public with a lot of <u>information</u>. (*correct*)

'Information' is an <u>uncountable</u> noun and thus remains invariable (unchanged) in its plural form.

Example 5
- My guidance teacher gives me <u>advices</u> on decorum everyday. (*wrong*)
- My guidance teacher gives me <u>advice</u> on decorum everyday. (*correct*)

'Advice' is an <u>uncountable</u> noun that remains unchanged in the plural form.

Example 6
- Mrs. Mojapelo bought many <u>furnitures</u> from Fair Deal after winning three million Rands at the Zama-Zama lottery. (*wrong*)
- Mrs. Mojapelo bought a lot of <u>furniture</u> from Fair Deal after winning three million Rands at the Zama-Zama lottery. (*correct*)

'Furniture' does not take <u>s</u> because it is an <u>uncountable</u> noun. However, it is correct to say 'pieces of furniture.'

It is necessary to sustain <u>number</u> all through the sentence when we write or speak in English. Errors often occur when the <u>verb</u> of a complex sentence does not agree with the <u>subject</u>. This happens when the sentence is complicated and it is difficult to find the subject and the main verb. Whether a verb is singular or plural is determined by the subject. The same <u>number</u> must be sustained throughout the sentence. Look at the following examples.

Example 1
- Neither of the brothers <u>were</u> very clever, but they made their way in the world by dint of hard work. (*wrong*)
- Neither of the brothers <u>was</u> very clever but <u>each</u> made his way in the world by dint of hard work. (*correct*)

In the first sentence the agreement between the verb and the subject is incorrect. When we use the word 'neither' the subjects are treated as <u>singular</u>.

Example 2
- Not everyone <u>think</u> that this government is taking crime seriously. (*wrong*)
- Not everyone <u>thinks</u> that this government is taking crime seriously. (*correct*)

We use <u>everyone</u> or <u>everybody</u> in the <u>singular</u> form to refer to all the people in a particular group (e.g. everyone in the street <u>was</u> shocked / when everyone <u>goes</u> home, etc).

Example 3
- This is not a job for <u>anyone</u> who <u>are</u> slow with figures. (*wrong*)
- This is not a job for <u>anyone</u> who <u>is</u> slow with figures. (*correct*)

Note that you use 'anyone' or 'anybody' to refer to a person when you are emphasizing that it could be any person out of a large number of people. It is always used in the singular.

Example 4
- If <u>anyone</u> <u>have</u> lost a big sum of money, please apply to the Lost Property Office and give full details of where and when the loss occurred. (*wrong*)
- If <u>anyone</u> <u>has</u> lost a big some of money, please apply to the Lost Property Office and give details of where and when the loss occurred. (*correct*)

Notice the concord between the subject of the sentence 'anyone' and the auxiliary verb has in the second sentence.

We shall discuss some common errors associated with nouns that remain <u>invariable</u> (unchanged) in the singular and plural forms. A sizeable number of scripts that teachers correct are replete with mistakes stemming from this aspect of English language grammar. A couple of examples would clarify the point.

Example 1
- I went to Spar to buy five dozens eggs. (*wrong*)
- I went to Spar to buy five dozen eggs. (*correct*)

When the word <u>dozen</u> is preceded by a numeral (e.g. <u>two</u>, <u>three</u>, <u>four</u>, <u>five</u>, etc.) the plural form should not be used. However, when <u>dozen</u> is not preceded by a numeral or by an indefinite article 'a' the plural form is used, e.g. <u>there were dozens of eggs at Spar</u>. (*correct*)

Example 2
- My mother used to give me good <u>advices</u> on sexuality. (*wrong*)
- My mother used to give me good <u>advice</u> on sexuality. (*correct*)

The first sentence is incorrect because the noun <u>advice</u> has been used in the plural form. When only one advice is meant, it is advisable to use the expression 'a piece of advice' e.g. <u>let me give you a good piece of advice on sexuality</u>.

Example 3
- <u>Informations</u> on census statistics <u>were</u> broadcast on national television yesterday. (*wrong*)
- <u>Information</u> on census statistics <u>was</u> broadcast on national television yesterday. (*correct*)

If reference is being made to only one thing, it is desirable to say 'an item of information.'

Example 4
- <u>Furnitures</u> are quite cheap at Geen and Richards. (*wrong*)
- <u>Furniture</u> is quite cheap at Geen and Richards. (*correct*)

Furniture is a <u>singular</u> noun that always takes a <u>singular</u> verb. Notice that it is acceptable to say 'a piece of furniture' which means 'one item of furniture only.'

Example 5
- My <u>luggages</u> got missing at the Harare International Airport. (*wrong*)
- My <u>luggage</u> got missing at the Harare International Airport. (*correct*)

<u>Luggage</u> cannot be used in the plural form because the singular form connotes plurality. 'Luggage' means the suitcases and bags that you take with you when you travel. It is noteworthy that <u>luggage</u> and <u>baggage</u> are synonyms. Like <u>luggage</u>, <u>baggage</u> does not take an 's' e.g. <u>the baggage is ready for the train</u>.

Example 6
- SAA has just bought fifty <u>aircrafts</u> from America. (*wrong*)
- SAA has just bought fifty <u>aircraft</u> from America. (*correct*)

The word <u>aircraft</u> (=aeroplane) remains invariable in the plural form. Grammatical errors caused by the misuse of 's' are quite frequent in English language communication. Teachers and pupils would do well to pay extra attention to <u>NUMBER</u> in English grammar.

We should revisit the problem of confusion in <u>number</u>, with particular emphasis on nouns that can take an 's' and thus change their meanings. These include: <u>fish</u>, <u>hair</u>, <u>thousand</u>, <u>fruit</u>, <u>damage</u>, <u>character</u>, <u>people</u>, etc. We shall use some examples to make this point clear.

Example 1

- Last night we ate <u>fishes</u> for dinner. (*wrong*)
- Last night we ate <u>fish</u> for dinner. (*correct*)

It should be noted that <u>fish</u> as flesh of fish eaten as <u>food</u> or in bulk (=large numbers) is always singular. The plural form <u>fishes</u> denotes fish individually or many species of fish. Example: I caught two large fishes yesterday. (*correct*)

Example 2
- That blonde has light brown <u>hairs</u>. (*wrong*)
- That blonde has light brown <u>hair</u>. (*correct*)

When the word "hair" is used to denote a single thread or strand (of hair), the plural form may be used. Example: I found several hairs in my food at the restaurant. (*correct*)

Example 3
- This hall can contain ten <u>thousands</u> people. (*wrong*)
- This hall can contain ten <u>thousand</u> people correct. (*correct*)

Words like <u>thousand, million</u>, and <u>hundred</u> take the plural form only if they are not preceded by a numeral. Example: <u>thousands</u> of people were present / <u>hundreds</u> of children died / <u>millions</u> of animals were sold.

Example 4
- We don't have <u>many fruits</u> in this locality. (*wrong*)
- We don't have <u>much fruit</u> in this locality. (*correct*)

The plural form <u>fruits</u> is rarely used in modern English. <u>Fruits</u> generally refers to various kinds of fruit; oranges, apricots, pears, apples and a host of others.

Example 5
- The accident caused <u>many damages</u> to property. (*wrong*)
- The accident caused <u>much damage</u> to property. (*correct*) The plural form 'damages' is acceptable usage when it refers to money paid to someone by somebody who has damaged their reputation or property. This is generally a court injunction. Example: he was vindicated in court and damages were awarded. (*correct*)

Example 6
- In school teachers strive to build good <u>characters</u>. (*wrong*)
- In school teachers strive to build good <u>character</u>. (*correct*) The plural form <u>characters</u> denotes the persons in a play or book. It may also be used in reference to the letters of the alphabet.

Example 7
- There are <u>many peoples</u> in the Pretoria train. (*wrong*)
- There are <u>many people</u> in the Pretoria train. (*correct*)

The plural <u>peoples</u> may be used to denote the different races or ethnic groups that make up a particular nation. Example: the native peoples of Southern Africa.

This lesson seeks to shed some light on the singular and plural forms of nouns. A noun is said to be singular (or in the singular number) if it refers to one thing. Example: book, tie, journey, etc. On the other hand, a noun is said to be plural (or in the plural number) when it refers to more than one thing. Example: books, ties, journeys, etc. Not all nouns take an <u>-s</u> in the plural form. Example: phenomenon-phenomena; addendum-addenda; datum-data; radius-radii.

Some nouns which end with a <u>-y</u> preceded by a consonant change the <u>-y</u> into <u>-ies</u> in the plural form. Example:ally-allies; country-countries; reply-replies.

However, nouns ending in <u>-y</u> preceded by a vowel usually take an <u>-s</u>. Example: ray-rays; jersey-jerseys; toy-toys; ploy-ploys. Generally, problems arise when speakers of English are faced with exceptions rather than the rule.

Example 1
- We paid a visit to the zoo and saw several animals: monkeys, cows, goats and <u>oxes</u>. (*wrong*)
- We paid a visit to the zoo and saw several animals: monkeys, cows, goats and <u>oxen</u>. (*correct*)

Some nouns have irregular plurals: ox-oxen; mouse-mice; goose-geese; tooth-teeth; etc.

Example 2
- This man looks really weird. He has <u>tattoes</u> all over his body. (*wrong*)
- This man looks really weird. He has <u>tattoos</u> all over his body. (*correct*)

Some nouns that end in -o and are of foreign origin form their plurals by taking an -s. Example: folio-folios; proviso-provisos; piano-pianos; tyro-tyros; solo-solos.

Example 3

- The little boy cut his finger with a scissors. (*wrong*)
- The little boy cut his finger with a pair of scissors. (*correct*)

Some nouns, because of their meaning, have no singular form. These include: scissors, trousers, dregs, binoculars, measles, etc.

Example 4
- The news were so bad that Nthabiseng fainted. (*wrong*)
- The news was so bad that Nthabiseng fainted. (*correct*)

Some words are plural nouns used as if they were singular. These include: news, politics, dynamics, innings, means, tidings, whereabouts, etc. Users of English should pay particular attention to the proper use of these words.

Errors stemming from non-agreement of verbs in number are frequent in daily speech. Teachers encounter similar problems in the classwork and assignments submitted by pupils. We have to spot these problems and correct them before they become part of their speech pattern.

Example 1
- The principal announced that a large supply of books are expected for the upcoming school year. (*wrong*)
- The principal announced that a large supply of books was expected for the upcoming school year. (*correct*)

When the subject is singular, the verb must be singular, and when the subject is plural, the verb must be plural as well. Care should be taken when a plural noun (e.g. books) comes between a singular subject (e.g. supply) and its verb. The subject of this sentence is supply, and not books.

Example 2
- Many teenagers lost their life while swimming at sea. (*wrong*)
- Many teenagers lost their lives while swimming at sea. (*correct*)

In English, words such as life, heart, soul, body and mind, are used in the plural form when they refer to more than one person.

Example 3
- This errors are made by foreigners learning to speak our native tongue. (*wrong*)
- These errors are make by foreigners learning to speak our native tongue. (*correct*)

This changes to these if the noun that follows is in the plural number as seen in the sentences above.

Example 4
- There is many pupils waiting to talk to the principal. (*wrong*)
- There are many pupils waiting to talk to the principal. (*correct*)

There is changes to there are if the noun that follows is the plural number.

EXERCISE 1
Provide the plural form of the nouns below.
a) hoof
b) turf
c) wharf
d) knife
e) cupful
f) passerby
g) secretary
h) crisis
i) thesis
j) analysist)
k) oasis
l) banjo
m) commando
n) gecho
o) atlas
p) larva
q) alibi
r) motto
s) cargo
  domino

EXERCISE 2
Give the plural form of the following borrowed words.
a) beau
b) plateau
c) bureau
d) madam
e) mister
f) focus
g) fungus
h) stimulus
i) stadium
j) phenomenon
k) louse
l) mouse
m) matrix
n) vortex
o) index
p) criterion
q) automaton
r) datum
s) memorandum
t) erratum

Chapter 22

Omissions

In this lesson we shall pinpoint some common mistakes in English resulting from unacceptable omissions. Errors of omission are frequent in essays and letters written by English second language speakers. That is why we deem it necessary to draw attention to these pitfalls.

Example 1
- I was born 23 December 1988. (*wrong*)
- I was born <u>on</u> 23 December 1988. (*correct*)

The preposition 'on' should have been used in the first sentence to show the date of birth of the speaker.

Example 2
- They live in shacks because they have no houses to live. (*wrong*)
- They live in shacks because they have no houses to live <u>in</u>. (*correct*)

It is imperative (necessary) to use the preposition 'in' after the verb 'live' because it is intransitive.

Example 3
- John's younger sister knows to play the piano very well. (*wrong*)
- John's younger sister knows <u>how</u> to play the piano very well. (*correct*)

It should be noted that after the verb 'to know' the verb that follows must be in the infinitive preceded by 'how.'

Example 4
- He ran lest he misses the train. (*wrong*)
- He ran lest he <u>should</u> miss the train. (*correct*)

The word 'lest' (= in order that...not) is generally followed by the auxiliary 'should.'

Example 5
- The head boy is more responsible than anybody. (*wrong*)
- The head boy is more responsible than anybody <u>else</u>. (*correct*)

In making a comparison between one person or thing and all others of the same kind, the word 'else' should be used after everybody, anybody, anything, etc.

Example 6
- The tourist admitted that he had never seen such a thing. (*wrong*)
- The tourist admitted that he had never seen such a thing before. (*correct*)

The word 'before' should not be left out in making a comparison between one thing and all others of the same kind.

Example 7
- Sipho boasted to us that he enjoyed during the holidays. (*wrong*)
- Sipho boasted to us that he enjoyed himself during the holidays. (*correct*) **OR**
- Sipho boasted to us that he enjoyed his holidays. (*correct*) The verb 'enjoy' cannot be followed by a preposition. It must always have an object which may be either a noun or reflective pronoun.

Example 8
- The unfortunate was arrested and put behind bars. (*wrong*)
- The unfortunate person was arrested and put behind bars. (*correct*)

Generally, a noun is omitted after an adjective only when the adjective is used as a collective noun. Example: the poor envy the rich.

Note that the idiomatic expression 'behind bars' means 'in prison.'

EXERCISE 1
Provide the missing words in the sentences below.

a) Bra Gibba was born 1994.

b) Summer the weather is very hot in this part of the world.

c) Christmas Day, Sandile received many gifts from friends.

d) Khoza and his wife arrived the Johannesburg International Airport at 3 p.m.

e) There is a conference in Nairobi October 15, 2000.

f) Msibi often returns home noon for lunch.

g) Winter the weather is terribly cold in South Africa.

h) The car will be brought back Tuesday.

i) Afternoon I will go and fetch the mail.
j) I bought this suit five thousand rands.

EXERCISE 2
Supply the words omitted from the sentences below.
a) Thiza, someone is knocking the door.
b) Tsepo is searching his lost book.
c) Ngwane explained me the problem very well.
d) Nakedi never listens her father.
e) Cosmas responded my question immediately.
f) Shandu is in a hurry, he cannot wait us.
g) Mbeki asked my calculator yesterday but hasn't returned it.
h) Njabulo pointed the lunatic and broke into a run.
i) Sithole was charged rape.
j) Pearl was accused stealing by her friends.

Chapter 23

Parts of Speech

In this lesson we shall dwell on some common errors in English attributable to the wrong substitution of one part of speech for another. The following examples would clarify the point.

Example 1
- I am cross with my teacher because he called me <u>a foolish</u>. (*wrong*)
- I am cross with my teacher because he called <u>a fool</u>. (*correct*)

Note that <u>foolish</u> is an adjective and cannot be substituted for the noun <u>fool</u>. It is, however, correct to say <u>a foolish person</u>. I am cross with my teacher because he called me a <u>foolish</u> <u>person</u>. (*correct*)

Example 2
- After the burglary, we found all the windows <u>opened</u>. (*wrong*)
- After the burglary, we found all the windows <u>open</u>. (*correct*)

Note that <u>open</u> is an adjective that qualifies the noun <u>windows</u> in the first sentence, whereas <u>opened</u> can be used as the <u>past</u> and <u>past participle</u> tenses of the infinitive <u>to open</u>. It is correct to say: The burglars <u>have opened</u> all the windows. **OR** The burglars <u>opened</u> all the windows.

Example 3
- This man is a terrible <u>liar</u>; he never speaks <u>true</u>. (*wrong*)
- This man is a terrible liar; he never <u>tells the truth</u>. (*correct*)

Notice that the word <u>true</u> is an adjective and is generally used to qualify something that is based on facts rather than being invented or imagined. Example: a true story, true democracy, etc. Conversely, the word <u>truth</u> is the noun form of the adjective <u>true</u>.

Example 4
- Your behaviour shows that you are a <u>coward</u> man. (*wrong*)
- Your behaviour shows that you are a <u>coward</u>. (*correct*) **OR**
- Your behaviour shows that you are <u>cowardly</u>. (*correct*) Note that coward (person without courage) is a noun. The adjective derived from this noun is <u>cowardly</u>. <u>Cowardice</u> (not <u>cowardness</u>) is cowardly behaviour.

Example 5
- It has been announced on radio that twenty persons are <u>died</u> following the ghastly accident. (*wrong*)
- It has been announced on radio that twenty persons are <u>dead</u> following the ghastly accident. (*correct*) **OR**
- It has been announced on radio that twenty persons <u>died</u> following the ghastly accident. (*correct*)

Example 6
- My father <u>does not afraid</u> of anyone. (*wrong*)
- My father does not <u>fear</u> any one. (*correct*) **OR**
- My father is not <u>afraid of</u> anyone. (*correct*)

I would like to stress that parts of speech constitute quite a troublesome aspect of the English language. Teachers and students of English would do well to dedicate ample time to the full mastery of this aspect of grammar.

In this lesson, I will be discussing frequent errors that English second language speakers commit by swapping one part of speech for another. At times speakers, even create words that are unacceptable in English. Example: <u>detailly</u>, <u>instalmentally</u>, <u>invitees</u>, etc.

Example 1
- President Thabo Mbeki has explained the concept of 'African Renaissance' <u>detailly</u>. (*wrong*)
- President Thabo Mbeki has explained the concept of 'African Renaissance' <u>in detail</u>. (*correct*)

If you discuss or explain something in detail, you do it thoroughly and carefully.

Example 2
- You are going to pay back this loan <u>instalmentally</u> over a period of ten years. (*wrong*)
- You are going to pay back this loan <u>in installments</u> over a period of ten years. (*correct*)

Notice that if you pay for something <u>in installments</u>, you pay small sums of money at regular intervals over a period of time.

Example 3
- This evening, we are hosting thirty <u>invitees</u> from Phalaborwa. (*wrong*)

- This evening, we are hosting thirty <u>guests</u> from Phalaborwa. (*correct*)

The expression 'invited guests' is acceptable in English as well.

Example 4
- Mosima will never stop <u>jealousing</u> her sister for marrying a rich man. (*wrong*)
- Mosima wil never stop <u>being jealous</u> of her sister for marrying a rich man.

Notice that 'jealous' is an adjective, and cannot be used as an action word (i.e. verb) as the speaker has done in sentence 1 above. 'Jealous' exists as a qualifier, not as a doing word.

Example 5
- The soldiers marched <u>disorderly</u> on Freedom Day. (*wrong*)
- The soldiers marched <u>in disorder</u> on Freedom Day. (*correct*)

<u>Disorderly</u> is an <u>adjective</u>, and cannot be used as an <u>adverb</u> as seen in sentence 1.

Example 6
- The committee was <u>chairmaned</u> by Mr. Ngoako. (*wrong*)
- The committee was <u>chaired</u> by Mr. Ngoako. (*correct*)

The word <u>chair</u> has replaced <u>chairman</u> in current English. The chair of a meeting or committee is the head.

EXERCISE 1

Some parts of speech have been wrongly used in the sentences below. Rewrite them correctly.

a) Anne-Marie said I was fool to accept such an offer.
b) Cohen is such a miser person.
c) Mr. Payne spent the entire afternoon lone.
d) Mr. Kirkegaard behaves friendly.
e) Mrs. Kamper is such a truly woman.
f) Lenjo's car worths R100 million.
g) The lame man does not able to climb the stairs.
h) Lebeloane has weighted the luggage.
i) Roger Miller plays soccer very good.
j) Awoonor sang quite beautiful this morning in church.

EXERCISE 2

Rewrite the following sentences correctly.

a) Do you not afraid of the lions?
b) The little boy has loss his ball.
c) The pupil has past his examination very well.
d) The athlete ran passed us.
e) He gave me a good piece of advise.
f) You was first to greet the professor.
g) The number of newspapers published in this country are increasing.
h) The poors say that money cannot buy happiness.
i) I am waiting for two hours now.
j) I have many works to do this night before going to bed.

Chapter 24

Prepositions

In this lesson, I will dwell on common errors in English that may be attributed to the unnecessary use of prepositions. As a reminder, a preposition is a word that shows a relationship between things or persons, usually where they are in relation to one another (e.g. <u>with</u>, <u>on</u>, <u>under</u>, <u>between</u>, <u>among</u>, <u>in front of</u>, etc.). A few examples would shed some more light on this point.

Example 1
- The teacher asked the entire class to answer <u>to</u> his question. (*wrong*)
- The teacher asked the entire class to answer his question. (*correct*)

The verb 'answer' (= give facts that are asked for) does not take the preposition 'to.' However, the noun 'answer' (= reply / response) does take the preposition 'to.' Example: His answer to my question was partly correct.

Example 2
- When we reached <u>at</u> the school, everyone had left. (*wrong*)
- When we reached the school, everyone had left. (*correct*) The verb 'reach' (= arrive at) does not take the preposition 'to.' Notice, however, that the verb 'arrive' does take 'at.' Example: <u>When we arrived at the school, everyone had left.</u> (*correct*)

Example 3
- The novel comprises of ten chapters. (*wrong*)
- The novel comprises ten chapters. (*correct*)

The verb <u>comprise</u> (= made up of) does not take the preposition 'of.' But the expression 'is comprised of' does take 'of.'

Example: <u>This novel is comprised of ten chapters.</u> (*correct*)

Example 4
- The three robbers hid behind <u>of</u> an old building. (*wrong*)
- The three robbers hid behind an old building. (*correct*) As in the previous example, the use of the preposition 'of' is unnecessary.

Example 5
- The armed bandits attacked <u>on</u> the cash-in-transit van. (*wrong*)
- The armed bandits attacked the cash-in-transit van. (*correct*)

Note that the use of the preposition <u>on</u> in the first sentence is unwarranted. However, the use of 'on' is acceptable in the expression 'make an attack on.' Example: <u>The armed bandits made an attack on the cash-in-transit van</u>. (*correct*)

Example 6
- The teacher ordered the noisy pupils to stand outside <u>of</u> the classroom. (*wrong*)
- The teacher ordered the noisy pupils to stand outside the classroom. (*correct*)

Example 7
- The Bible says that we must obey <u>to</u> our parents. (*wrong*)
- The Bible says that we must obey our parents. (*correct*) The verb 'obey' (= do what you are told) is generally not followed by the preposition 'to.' Example: <u>Obey the law</u> / <u>obey a command</u> / <u>obey an instruction</u>, etc.

Example 8
- The workers were fighting to enter <u>in</u> the car. (*wrong*)
- The workers were lighting to enter the car. (*correct*)

The verb 'enter' does not correlate with the preposition 'to' in all instances, for example, <u>enter a room</u>, <u>building</u>, <u>car</u>, etc.

It should be noted, however, that enter may be used in a number of idiomatic expressions to convey specific meanings. Example: <u>enter into a conversation</u>, <u>debate</u>, <u>discussion</u>, etc.

In this lesson we will focus attention on the challenges of English prepositions. Prepositions constitute such a vast and complex aspect of English that one can hardly boast knowing English until one is able to handle the intricacies that prepositions have in store.

Example 1
- We shall <u>round up</u> this lesson by doing some exercises on prepositions. (*wrong*)
- We shall <u>round off</u> this lesson by doing some exercises on prepositions. (*correct*)

Note that the first sentence is incorrect because the speaker has used the wrong preposition after the verb 'to round.' Round up and round off convey totally different meanings in English.

Round up: If the police or army round up a number of people, they arrest them.

Round off: If you round off an activity with something, you end that activity by doing something.

Example 2
- The police have <u>succeeded to</u> arrest the cash-in-transit robber. (*wrong*)
- The police have <u>succeeded in</u> arresting the cash-in-transit robber. (*correct*)

The first sentence is wrong because the speaker has used the wrong preposition after the verb 'succeeded.' 'Succeed' is usually followed by the preposition 'in' and a verb in the present participle tense.

Example 3
- We are all bound to <u>comply to</u> all the rules of this game. (*wrong*)
- We are all bound to <u>comply with</u> all the rules of this game. (*correct*)

The first sentence is incorrect because the verb <u>comply</u> does not correlate with the preposition 'to.' Usually, you <u>comply with</u> rules, regulations, or requirements. But you <u>conform to</u> them.

Both expressions mean: <u>behave in the way that you are expected or supposed to behave</u>.

Example 4
- The conflict <u>resulted to</u> a bloody war. (*wrong*)
- The conflict <u>resulted in</u> a bloody war. (*correct*)

The verb <u>result</u> followed by the preposition <u>in</u> means <u>lead to</u> or <u>cause</u>.

Example 5
- These two pupils <u>come always</u> to school by bus. (*wrong*)
- These two pupils <u>always come</u> to school by bus. (*correct*)

Notice that the first sentence is wrong because adverbs of <u>indefinite time</u>, namely <u>always</u>, <u>ever</u>, <u>never</u>, <u>often</u>, <u>sometimes</u>, etc. are generally placed before the principal verb. However, with the verb 'to be' the adverb of indefinite time is placed after the verb. Example: They <u>always are</u> early. (*wrong*) They <u>are</u> <u>always</u> early. (*correct*)

Example 6
- I <u>last night</u> went to the gym. (*wrong*)
- I went to the gym <u>last night</u>. (*correct*)

Adverbs or adverbial phrases of <u>definite time</u>, like <u>yesterday</u>, <u>today</u>, <u>tomorrow</u>, <u>last week</u>, <u>last night</u>, <u>two months ago</u>, etc. are usually placed at the end of the sentence. However, if the speaker wishes to put emphasis on the time, he may place the adverb at the beginning of the sentence. Example: <u>Last night</u> I went to the gym. (*correct*) <u>Yesterday</u> I went to the movie. (*correct*)

Example 7
- I have read the <u>two first</u> chapters of this bestseller. (*wrong*)
- I have read the <u>first two</u> chapters of this bestseller. (*correct*)

The first sentence is incorrect because ordinal numerals (first, second, third, etc.) should come before cardinal numbers (one, two, three, etc.). The wrong positioning of <u>ordinal</u> and <u>cardinal</u> numbers in the first sentence makes it not only incorrect but also illogical. There cannot be two <u>first</u> chapters in one and the same book! Similarly, it is unacceptable to say: the <u>three last</u> chapters of the bestseller. Say: the <u>last three</u> chapters of the bestseller.

Example 8
- I showed <u>to Jonas</u> some of my stamps. (*wrong*)
- I showed some of my photos <u>to Jonas</u>. (*correct*)

Note that the first sentence is incorrect because the speaker has misplaced the indirect object <u>Jonas</u>.

Example 9
- The teacher asked me why was I absent on Friday. (*wrong*)
- The teacher asked me why I was absent on Friday. (*correct*)

Users of English should always pay particular attention to what they say and write in order to avoid errors arising from the wrong positioning of adverbs, conjunctions, prepositions, clauses, numerals, articles and participles.

Example 10
- The MEC pointed out that he <u>provided them</u> enough funds for the project. (*wrong*)

- The MEC pointed out that he <u>provided them with</u> enough funds for the project. (*correct*)

Provide (= make available to) is generally followed by the preposition 'with.'

Example 11
- The government ought to supply schools enough textbooks. (*wrong*)
- The government ought to supply schools <u>with</u> enough textbooks. (*correct*)

Supply 'with' and 'provide with' are synonymous.

Example 12
- I do occasionally ask a favour from Mrs. Essa. (*wrong*)
- I do not occasionally ask Mrs. Essa to do me a favour. (*correct*)

OR

- I do occasionally ask a favour of Mrs. Essa. (*correct*)

Example 13
- My attorney has advised me to attach the letter <u>with</u> my case file. (*wrong*)
- My attorney has advised me to attach the letter <u>to</u> my case file. (*correct*) **OR**
- My attorney has advised me to enclose the letter <u>in</u> my case file. (*correct*)

Note that <u>to be attached to someone</u> means you are <u>very</u> fond of them. Example: She is very attached to her family.

Example 14
- The Premier came in person to congratulate the soccer team <u>in</u> their victory. (*wrong*)
- The Premier came in person to congratulate the soccer team <u>on</u> their victory. (*correct*)

'Congratulate' (=praise someone for something admirable) is generally followed by the preposition <u>on</u>. Sometimes it is followed by 'for.' Example: I really must congratulate the organizers <u>for</u> a job well done.

Example 15
- I would like to <u>avail</u> this opportunity to meet the Minister. (*wrong*)

- I would like to <u>avail myself</u> of this opportunity to meet the Minister. (*correct*)

'Avail oneself' of an opportunity means 'use' the opportunity.

EXERCISE 1

The double use of compound prepositions in the sentences below has led to verbosity (use of unnecessary words).

Rewrite the sentences correctly.

a) He invited us for the purpose of discussing the match fixtures.

b) I was lucky inasmuch as my friend was living in France and spoke French fluently.

c) The department is reviewing its policy with regard to immunization.

d) This is a question that has been asked several times in relation to our foreign policy.

e) I am calling with regard to your article on media racism.

f) The suit cost me in the region of R1OOO.

g) Taken in connection with its context, your statement has a deep meaning.

h) There is much anger in some quarters in connection with the situation as regards the inadequate supply of meat.

i) You need to resolve this problem as a matter of urgency.

j) Most parents are generally helpless with respect to the sexual behaviour of their children.

EXERCISE 2

Fill in the omitted prepositions in the expressions below.

a) To go_a sight-seeing trip.

b) To make the best of the time_one's disposal.

c) To travel____one's own risk.

d) To go_a conducted tour.

e) To take a look_a hotel guide.

f) To book accommodation____advance.

g) To be tired____waiting.

h) To undertake an extensive tour____the country.

i) To admire works____art at leisure.

j) To obtain a temporary visa___enter a country.

Chapter 25

Pronouns

All too often, mistakes are made by non-native speakers of English as a result of wrong use of <u>pronouns</u>. A <u>pronoun</u> is a word that replaces a noun. Pronouns are used in order to avoid repeating nouns. For example, you wouldn't say 'Joyce said Joyce would pay me a visit.' You would say 'Joyce said <u>she</u> would pay one a visit.'

The pronoun group englobes <u>personal pronouns</u>, (I, he, she, it, we, you, they), <u>possessive pronouns</u>, (mine, his, hers, ours, yours, theirs), <u>reflexive pronouns</u> (myself, yourself, himself, herself, itself, ourselves, yourselves, themselves), <u>relative</u> pronouns (who, which, that, whom), <u>indefinite pronouns</u> (anybody, anyone, anything, everyone, nobody, nothing, etc.)

Example 1
- Matsimela's father <u>he</u> works at the SABC. (*wrong*)
- Matsimela's father works at the SABC. (*correct*)

In sentence 1 above, the personal pronoun 'he' is redundant because it is synonymous with 'father.'

Example 2
- Though Docan and Lynette are husband and wife, they do not love themselves. (*wrong*)
- Though Docan and Lynette are husband and wife, they do not love <u>each other</u>. (*correct*)

The use of the reflexive pronoun 'themselves' in sentence 1 does not convey the idea of <u>reciprocity</u> which is implied in 'each other.' Note that 'each other' is a reciprocal pronoun. So also is 'one another.'

Example 3
- I was scandalised by all <u>what</u> I heard. (*wrong*)
- I was scandalised by all <u>that</u> I heard. (*correct*)

The use of <u>what</u> in sentence 1 is unacceptable. After the word <u>all</u>, it is correct to use <u>that</u>, not <u>what</u>. The English say 'all that,' not 'all what.'

Example 4
- The old woman <u>who she</u> greeted you is my granny. (*wrong*)
- The old woman <u>who</u> greeted you is my granny. (*correct*) The relative pronoun 'who' is the subject of the verb <u>greeted</u>. It is pointless to include a second subject 'she.'

Example 5
- The man <u>who</u> we bypassed is a witchdoctor. (*wrong*)
- The man we bypassed is a witchdoctor. (*correct*) **OR**
- The man <u>whom</u> we bypassed is a witchdoctor. (*correct*)

In spoken English, it is not wrong to omit the relative pronoun <u>who</u> as seen in sentence 2.

In this lesson, I will be discussing ways and means of avoiding mistakes that arise when speakers of English repeat the subject by using a <u>pronoun</u> after the noun. Look at these examples:

Example 1
- My younger brother <u>he</u> is attending school at Meridian College Pietersburg. (*wrong*)
- My younger brother is attending school at Meridian College Pietersburg. (*correct*)

It is not necessary to use the pronoun 'he' to denote the same person 'younger brother.' One or other may be used as the subject, but not both.

Example 2
- My auntie <u>she</u> is a nurse. (*wrong*)
- My auntie is a nurse. (*correct*)

The first sentence is unacceptable because the speaker has used the pronoun 'she' to denote the same person 'auntie.' This repetition is unwarranted.

Example 3
- Ntsako, who is a careless pupil, <u>he</u> lost his school bag. (*wrong*)
- Ntsako, who is a careless pupil, lost his school bag. (*correct*) If the <u>subordinate clause</u> is an enlargement of the subject, the <u>personal pronoun</u>, should not be used before the verb of the <u>principal clause</u> as seen in the second sentence above.

Example 4
- I went to Shoprite and <u>I</u> bought some fruit. (*wrong*)
- I went to Shoprite and bought some fruit. (*correct*)

In a compound sentence like the one above, the same subject is expressed once only. It should not be repeated for each verb.

Example 5
- The book <u>that</u> I lost <u>it</u> was old. (*wrong*)
- The book that I lost was old. (*correct*)

A <u>personal</u> as well as a <u>relative</u> pronoun cannot be used in the relative clause if they both refer to the same antecedent. In the first sentence, 'that' and 'it' both refer to book. This repetition is unnecessary.

Example 6
- I bought a French book to read <u>it</u>. (*wrong*)
- I bought a French book to read. (*correct*)

The first sentence is wrong because the speaker has repeated the object of the sentence with the infinitive. An object cannot be repeated with an infinitive of purpose if the verb takes an object.

This lesson centres on common errors in written and spoken English stemming from the wrong use of relative pronouns in adjectival clauses. It is noteworthy that relative pronouns --- <u>who</u>, <u>whom</u>, <u>which</u>, and <u>that</u> used to begin adjectival clauses must agree in number with the nouns to which they refer, as in the following examples:

Example 1
- He is one of the men who <u>was</u> arrested by the police. (*wrong*)
- He is one of the men who <u>were</u> arrested by the police. (*correct*)

The first sentence is wrong because there is wrong concord. The <u>who</u> relative pronoun refers to <u>men</u> and <u>men</u> is a plural noun; so <u>who</u> must be plural as well and should be followed by the <u>plural</u> verb <u>were</u> and not the <u>singular</u> verb <u>was</u>.

Example 2
- This is one of the boxes that <u>was</u> stolen. (*wrong*)
- This is one of the boxes that were <u>stolen</u>. (*correct*)

It should be noted that the first sentence is incorrect because, the <u>that</u> relative pronoun refers to <u>boxes</u> which is a plural noun and so should be followed by the plural verb <u>are</u> as seen in the second sentence.

Example 3
- This is the lady <u>who</u> I saw leaving the house. (*wrong*)

- This is the lady <u>whom</u> I saw leaving the house. (*correct*) The second sentence is correct because the relative pronoun <u>whom</u> is the object of the verb <u>saw</u> in the adjectival clause 'whom I saw leaving the house' and so we use the objective form of the pronoun <u>who</u> (i.e. <u>whom</u>).

Example 4
- Moloto and <u>me</u> went to the cinema last night. (*wrong*)
- Moloto and <u>I</u> went to the cinema last night. (*correct*)

All too often, speakers of English are confused as regards concord when there is a <u>double</u> subject (i.e. two pronouns or a noun and a pronoun). It should be noted that whether the pronoun is the complete subject or only part of it, it should always be in the <u>nominative</u> case.

Example 5
- It was <u>me</u> who broke the mirror. (*wrong*)
- It was <u>I</u> who broke the mirror. (*correct*)

Notice that the verb 'to be' in all its forms (i.e. <u>am</u>, <u>is</u>, <u>are, was, have been, will be</u>) is always followed by pronouns in the <u>nominative case</u> as seen in the second sentence above.

Example 6
- It is <u>them</u> who are refusing to vote for the ANC. (*wrong*)
- It is <u>they</u> who are refusing to vote for the ANC. (*correct*) The first sentence is incorrect because the pronoun <u>them</u> is in the <u>accusative case</u> and not the <u>nominative case</u>.

Many mistakes made by non-native speakers of English are attributable to confusion of pronouns. English language teachers would do well to treat this aspect of grammar succinctly.

In this lesson, we shall dwell on misused relative pronouns in English. <u>Which</u> is a relative pronoun used in reference to non-humans (i.e. animals and objects). Conversely, <u>who</u> is the correct relative pronoun to use when reference is being made to persons. By the same token, it is desirable to use <u>whose</u> and <u>whom</u> for persons. Let's see how these pronouns are frequently confused by English language speakers.

Example 1
- I have a brother <u>which</u> schools at Meridian College in Pietersburg. (*wrong*)

- I have a brother <u>who</u> schools at Meridian College in Pietersburg. (*correct*)

<u>Which</u> is not acceptable in the first sentence because <u>brother</u> is a human being.

Example 2
- I have understood all <u>what</u> you said. (*wrong*)
- I have understood all <u>that</u> you said. (*correct*)

The relative <u>what</u> cannot be used after words like <u>all, some, any, something, everything, anything, much, little</u>, and <u>nothing</u>. Only the relative pronoun <u>that</u> may be used after such words.

Sometimes, you may omit <u>that</u> entirely without doing damage to the meaning of the utterance (e.g. I have understood all you said).

Example 3
- I have seen the man <u>whom</u> you said is a rapist. (*wrong*)
- I have seen the man <u>who</u> you said is a rapist. (*correct*)

Example 4
- This is a woman <u>who</u> I know you can trust. (*wrong*)
- This is a woman <u>whom</u> I know you can trust. (*correct*) In the second sentence <u>whom</u> is the object of <u>you can trust</u>. <u>I know</u> is a mere parenthesis.

Example 5
- I like to help those <u>who</u> I love and <u>who</u> I know love me. (*wrong*)
- I like to help those <u>whom</u> I love and <u>whom</u> I know love me. (*correct*)

Example 6
- I cannot recall all <u>what</u> the teacher taught last week. (*wrong*)
- I cannot recall all <u>that</u> the teacher taught last week. (*correct*)

Example 7
- This is the girl <u>whom</u> we thought had been kidnapped. (*wrong*)
- This is the girl <u>who</u> we thought had been kidnapped. (*correct*)

Example 8
- The girl to <u>who</u> you spoke is my step-sister. (*wrong*)
- The girl to <u>whom</u> you spoke is my step-sister. (*correct*)

Example 9
- About <u>who</u> were you talking? (*wrong*)
- About <u>whom</u> were you talking? (*correct*)

Example 10
- <u>Whom</u> did you say won the prize? (*wrong*)
- <u>Who</u> did you say won the prize? (*correct*)

Example 11
- <u>What</u> do you find easier, English or French? (*wrong*)
- <u>Which</u> do you find easier, English or French? (correct)

This lesson focuses on common mistakes made by speakers of English as a result of poor understanding of the function of <u>relative pronouns</u> in English grammar.

Example 1
- This is the man <u>which</u> is accused of raping the granny. (*wrong*)
- This is the man <u>who</u> is accused of raping the granny. (*correct*)

<u>Which</u> is a <u>relative pronoun</u> that is used in reference to animals or things. The correct pronouns to use for persons are <u>who</u>, <u>whose</u> and <u>whom</u>. In some cases, <u>that</u> as a relative pronoun is acceptable.

Example 2
- I simply ignored all <u>what</u> they said to me. (*wrong*)
- I simply ignored all <u>that</u> they said to me. (*correct*)

Example 3
- I was introduced to the woman <u>whom</u> you said was a diplomat. (*wrong*)
- I was introduced to the woman <u>who</u> you said was a diplomat. (*correct*)

Example 4
- This is the best soccer match <u>which</u> I have ever watched. (*wrong*)
- This is the best soccer match <u>that</u> I have ever watched. (*correct*)

The relative pronoun that (not <u>who</u>, <u>whom</u> or <u>which</u> should be used after a superlative, e.g. <u>best</u>). However it may be omitted. This is the best soccer match I have ever watched. (*correct*)

EXERCISE 1
Choose the correct pronoun from the pair in brackets.
a) Let (he/him) and (she/her) go to the movie.
b) Jeanne wished (we/us) a safe journey.
c) Roselyn made (they/them) repeat the sentence thrice.
d) All the panellists greed except (he/him).
e) I knew the girl to be (her/she).

f) Those like (him/he) are always getting in trouble.
g) Javas did better than (me/I) this time.
h) Hazel likes you more than (me/I).
i) Basil and Nomsa ran faster than (we/us).
j) Mthembu gave you less than (she/her).

EXERCISE 2

Complete the following sentences with an appropriate pronoun chosen from these four: who, whom, that, which.

a) Mashoeng is the man___they thought was a thief.
b) Is she the girl___you think is a spy?
c) Nkosi is the lady_____they believe I am going to marry.
d) That is the wife of the man___was injured.
e) The child next to_____you are sitting is very ill.
f) Is it Mary-Jane's car___was stolen?
g) This is the problem___we have to solve urgently.
h) All animals___graze on fynbos are usually healthy.
i) Titanic was the best film_____I had ever watched.
j) This is the best thriller_I have read in my life.

Chapter 26

Punctuation Marks

This lesson focuses on the use of punctuation marks. An effective speaker uses pauses to group words together. In speech, we instinctively pause to provide clarity, precision and variety of tone.

In writing, we have two aids available to us, namely the appropriate choice of word order and the appropriate choice of punctuation marks. There are twelve punctuation marks in English: comma, semicolon, colon, full stop, question mark, exclamation mark, ellipsis dots, dash, hyphen, brackets, inverted commas (or quotation marks) and apostrophe.

Perhaps it is important to stress that the use of capital letters is generally considered a vital component of punctuation in English. Capital letters are used at the beginning of a sentence, direct speech, line of verse, book title, proper nouns, titles of persons, initials, abbreviations, etc.

Example 1
- Ayob would you please pass the salt and pepper. (*wrong*)
- Ayob, would you please pass the salt and pepper? (*correct*)

Note the use of the comma and question mark in sentence 2 above.

Example 2
- The study-guide a handsomely produced book provides tips on how to prepare for the exam. (*wrong*)
- The study-guide (a handsomely produced book) provides tips on how to prepare for the exam. (*correct*)

Note that instead of brackets, commas or dashes could be used to put 'a handsomely-produced book' in apposition.

Example 3
- We met a young australian in pretorius street on tuesday she told us she was looking for union buildings. (*wrong*)
- We met a young Australian in Pretorius Street on Tuesday. She told us she was looking for Union Buildings. (*correct*)

Example 4
- What a strange looking man. (*wrong*)
- What a strange-looking man! (*correct*)

Note the use of the hyphen in the compound adjective 'strange-looking' as well as the exclamation mark.

Example 5
- It won't cost much to repair the damage or so they say. (*wrong*)
- It won't cost much to repair the damage--or so they say. (*correct*)

The proper use of punctuation marks in writing ensure the following:

1) clarity;
2) precision;
3) variety of tone; and
4) variety of pause.

In speech, a speaker may 'punctuate' by using voice pitch, modulation, pace and tone; thus enhancing speech quality.

EXERCISE 1
Read the extract below and punctuate it properly.

Hear how kind mr Bons is. said his mother while his father said, very well. Let him say his poem, and that will do. He is going away to my sister on tuesday and she will cure him of his alley- slopering (laughter). Say your poem. the boy began. Standing aloof in giant ignorance. His father laughed again—roared. One for you, my son! Standing aloof in giant ignorance! I never knew these poets talked sense Just describes you. Here, Bons, you go in for poetry. put him through it will you, while I Fetch the whisky.

Yes give me the Keats said Mr Bons. Let him say his keats to me So for a very short moment the wise man and the ignorant boy were left alone in the smoking room.

Standing aloof in ignorance of these I dream and of the Cyclades as one who sits ashore and longs perchance to visit— Quite right To visit what?

To visit dolphin coral in deep seas said the boy, and burst into tears.

Come, come! why do you cry

Because—because all these words that only rhymed before, now that I've come back they're me. Mr Bons laid the Keats down.

The case was more interesting than he had expected. You? he exclaimed. This sonnet you? Yes—and look further on: Aye, on the shores of darkness there is light, and precipices show untrodden green. It is so Sir. All these things are true.

I never doubted it, said Mr bons, with closed eyes. You—then you believe me?

You believe in the omnibus and the driver and the storm that return ticket I got for nothing and — Tut, tut! No more of your yarns my boy. I meant that I never doubted the essential truth of poetry. Some day when you have read more you will understand what I mean.

But Mr bons it is so. There is light upon the shores of darkness. I have seen it coming. Light and a wind. Nonsense, said Mr Bons. (*E. M. Forster*)

<u>EXERCISE 2</u>

Punctuate the following sentences.

a) Kere was so tired that he could not walk
b) Why did Bongani go to bed so early
c) You can go wherever you want said my mother
d) I wonder where Fabian could be now
e) I don't know the house in which Simphiwe was born
f) What the hell is going on here
g) These are the shoes that Sonnyboy wore on Sunday
h) Mike went to spar and bought some foodstuff rice, mealie, potatoes, and meat
i) Which train goes to grahamstown
j) each player will receive a cash prize of R30,000

Chapter 27

Quantifiers

In this lesson we shall be discussing some errors that arise from the wrong use of <u>quantifiers</u> in English. <u>Quantities</u> and <u>amounts</u> are sometimes referred to by using words such as <u>several</u>, <u>some</u>, <u>a lot</u>, <u>much</u>, <u>a number of</u>, <u>most</u>, etc. linked to the noun group.
Such words and phrases are called <u>quantifiers</u>.

Example 1
- Some of the information <u>have</u> already been analysed. (*wrong*)
- Some of the information <u>has</u> already been analysed. (*correct*)

When you use a quantifier as the <u>object</u> of a verb, you must use a singular verb form if the noun group that follows is in the singular or uncountable form.

Example 2
- Lots of evidence given by the witness <u>are</u> inaccurate. (*wrong*)
- Lots of evidence given by the witness <u>is</u> inaccurate. (*correct*)

Note that when the quantifier <u>lots of</u> is used with an uncountable noun or a singular noun group as the subject of the verb, the verb is singular, though the quantifier sounds plural.

Example 3
- Tons of money <u>were</u> spent on the white elephant project. (*wrong*)
- Tons of money <u>was</u> spent on the white elephant project. (*correct*)

The quantifier <u>tons of</u> is used with an uncountable noun <u>money</u> and should take a singular verb as seen in sentence 2.

Example 4
- Heaps of experience <u>are</u> needed for this kind of job. (*wrong*)
- Heaps of experience <u>is</u> needed for this kind of job. (*correct*)

<u>Heaps of</u> or <u>a heap of</u> something is a large quantity of it. This quantifier takes a singular verb.

Example 5
- Loads of embarrassing evidence <u>have</u> been produced to prove the teacher's guilt. (*wrong*)

- Loads of embarrassing evidence <u>has</u> been produced to prove the teacher's guilt. (*correct*)

<u>Loads of</u>, <u>heaps of</u>, <u>lots of</u>, <u>tons of</u>, and a host of other quantifiers are colloquial expressions that should be restricted to informal communication.

In this lesson, we shall discuss some more errors stemming from the wrong use of quantifiers in English, namely <u>few</u>, <u>a few</u>, <u>each</u>, <u>every</u>, <u>little</u> and <u>a little</u>. Generally, <u>few</u> is used to show that only a small number of persons or things are being referred to. You may use <u>too</u> and <u>very</u> in front of <u>few</u>, e.g. she has <u>few</u> friends / <u>few</u> militants plan to vote for the ANC / very <u>few</u> companies collect taxes. Some erroneous usages of these quantifiers include:

Example 1

- Although the question was easy, <u>a few</u> candidates answered it correctly. (*wrong*)
- Although the question was easy, <u>few</u> candidates answered it correctly. (*correct*)

<u>Few</u> means not many and emphasises the smallness of the number of candidates who answered the questions correctly. It is distinguished from <u>a few</u> which denotes <u>at least</u> some. Notice that the difference between <u>few</u> and <u>a few</u> is quite subtle but significant.

Example 2

- After the violent storm <u>a few</u> of the beach houses still had roofs on. (*wrong*)
- After the violent storm, <u>few</u> of the beach houses still had roofs on. (*correct*)

Example 3

- <u>Every</u> one of the two sisters anxiously awaited the exam results. (*wrong*)
- <u>Each</u> one of the two sisters anxiously awaited the exam results. (*correct*)

<u>Each</u> is used for one of two or more persons or things taken one by one. <u>Every</u> is always used for more than two persons or things taken as a group. <u>Each</u> is a more <u>individual</u> and <u>specific</u> word, whereas <u>every</u> is an emphatic word.

Example 4

- The two lovers hugged and kissed <u>one another</u> passionately. (*wrong*)
- The two lovers hugged and kissed <u>each other</u> passionately. (*correct*)

You use <u>one another</u> in reference to a group in order to indicate that each member of the group does something to or for the other members. On the contrary, <u>each other</u> is used in reference to only two persons or things, to indicate that one person or thing does something to the other or has a particular connection with the other.

Example 5
- He slept <u>a little</u> and left worse the following day. (*wrong*)
- He slept <u>little</u> and felt worse the following day. (*correct*) Little means <u>not much</u> and emphasises the smallness of an amount or quantity. It is distinguished from <u>a little</u> which means <u>at least some</u>.

Example 6
- He is very ill; there is <u>a little</u> hope for him. (*wrong*)
- He is very ill; there is <u>little</u> hope for him. (*correct*)

Example 7
- We must save <u>little</u> money for our journey to Cape Town. (*wrong*)
- We must save <u>a little</u> money for our journey to Cape Town. (*correct*)

Example 8
- I cannot afford it as I have <u>a little</u> money left. (*wrong*)
- I cannot afford it as I have <u>little</u> money left. (*correct*) Speakers of English, especially students, are advised to pay particular attention to the use of these and other quantifiers in their essays and letters in order to avoid gaffes.

This lesson focuses on some quantitative adverbs that are frequently confused by non-native speakers of English, notably <u>many</u>, <u>much</u>, <u>too much</u>, <u>very much</u>.

Example 1
- My younger sister likes the cinema <u>too much</u>. (*wrong*)
- My younger sister likes the cinema <u>very much</u>. (*correct*) The first sentence is incorrect because the speaker has used <u>too</u> which means <u>more than enough</u>. <u>Very</u> is acceptable because it makes the

adverb <u>much</u> stronger. <u>Very much</u> is used instead of <u>much</u> for greater emphasis.

Example 2
- My elder brother is too much stronger than I am. (wrong)
- My elder brother is very much stronger than I am. (correct)

As mentioned above, the expression <u>very much</u> is generally used for emphatic purposes. This is why the first sentence is wrong and the second correct. <u>Too much</u> denotes an excessive quantity or degree. Example: He drank <u>too much</u> and became ill.

Example 3
- I was <u>too much</u> afraid of the police dog. (*wrong*)
- I was <u>very</u> afraid of the police dog. (*correct*) **OR**
- I was <u>very much</u> afraid of the police dog. (*correct*)

<u>Very</u> is used with adjectives and adverbs in the <u>positive degree</u>. Conversely, <u>much</u> is used with adjectives and adverbs in the <u>comparative degree</u>.

Example 4
- My mother was <u>too much</u> astonished at the terrible news. (*wrong*)
- My mother was <u>very much</u> astonished at the terrible news. (*correct*)

Example 5
- I am <u>very much tired</u>, let's call it a day. (*wrong*)
- I am <u>very tired</u>, let's call it a day. (*correct*)

Some adjectives and past participles that are used in the sense of adjectives may take <u>very</u> before them. Example: I am <u>very</u> pleased to meet you.

Example 6
- The novel my father bought for me is <u>very much</u> interesting. (*wrong*)
- The novel my father bought for me is <u>very</u> interesting. (*correct*)

Example 7
- It is now <u>very hot</u> to play soccer. (*wrong*)
- It is now <u>too hot</u> to play. (*correct*)

Example 8
- In Pietersburg, it is <u>too hot</u> in summer. (*wrong*)

- In Pietersburg, it is <u>very hot</u> in summer. (*correct*)

Example 9
- My cousin hasn't <u>much</u> books. (*wrong*)
- My cousin hasn't <u>many</u> books. (*correct*)

Example 10
- There <u>is too many</u> dust on my desk. (*wrong*)
- There is <u>too much</u> dust on my desk. (*correct*)

<u>Many</u> is used with plural <u>countable</u> nouns whereas <u>much</u> is used with singular <u>collective</u> nouns (e.g. water, oil, bread, etc.).

EXERCISE 1

Fill the blank spaces with either <u>very</u> or <u>much</u>.

a) Enoch is_____angry because you did not come to his party yesterday.

b) Sontonga was_pleased to meet the president.

c) Yvonne was___afraid of being raped.

d) That was a____amusing tale.

e) Thembi looks_tired today.

f) Ernest plays___better than his opponents.

g) Bongi's essay is worse than mine.

h) Brian was____interested to hear the outcome of the match.

i) Nomonde was_astonished at the news.

j) That was a____meaningful poem.

EXERCISE 2

Choose <u>very much</u> or <u>too much</u> to fill the blank spaces.

a) Mohammed likes grapes_____.

b) We cannot study in this room, there is noise.

c) Fifty rands is__for this book.

d) Cindy drank___at the party and felt sick the following day.

e) Chester talks___; he is a chatterbox.

f) We were_____amazed to hear that he died suddenly.

g) Ndoumbe is___obliged to you.

h) Thank you____for the service you've rendered us.

i) Gugu was_____interested in AIDS education.

j) Ngema has helped me_.

Chapter 28

Reported Speech

In this lesson, I would like to discuss the importance of reported speech in the English language. The conversion of direct speech (i.e. the actual words of a speaker) into reported speech (an account of what someone has said) is not a difficult process but mistakes are often made because speakers of English do not always know what to do or what is required of them. It should be noted that when we wish to change direct into reported (indirect) speech, we have to alter it slightly so that we are not using the actual words of the speaker. We repeat what someone else has said more or less in our own words but conveying as near as possible the correct sense of what was said.

Example 1 Direct Speech:
- "I will return to Cape Town tomorrow," my father said.

Reported Speech:
- My father said that he will return to Cape Town tomorrow. (*wrong*)
- My father said that he <u>would</u> return to Cape Town the <u>next day</u>. (*correct*)

Note that reported speech is always introduced by a verb of saying: asked, inquired, observed, said, remarked, answered, etc. (always in the past tense) followed by 'that' used as a conjunction as seen in the example above.

Example 2 Direct Speech:
- "Has the train for Johannesburg left?" Canisius Niba asked.

Reported Speech
- Canisius Niba asked whether the train for Johannesburg <u>has</u> left. (*wrong*)
- Canisius Niba asked whether the train for Johannesburg <u>had</u> left. (*correct*) **OR**
- Canisius Niba <u>wished</u> to know whether the train for Johannesburg <u>had</u> left. (*correct*)

Reported speech involves repeating something that was said in the past. It must therefore be put in the <u>past tense</u>. If it is in the <u>past</u>

tense in the direct speech, it must be put in the past perfect tense in the reported speech.

Example 3 Direct Speech:
- "Release these men now," the captain said.

Reported Speech:
- The captain ordered that these men should be released now. (*wrong*)
- The captain ordered that those men should be released at that moment. (*correct*)
- The captain ordered (him, them or us) to release those men then. (*correct*)

In the reported speech, all words of nearness (e.g. adverbs of place and time) are usually altered to words of remoteness. (e.g. now becomes then or at that moment, these becomes those, etc.).

This lesson seeks to shed some light on the correct use of interrogative sentences in indirect speech. An interrogative sentence asks a question. It is different from a declarative sentence that states a fact or an imperative sentence that gives a command.

In indirect (reported) speech, you relate what someone else has said. This is different from direct speech where the actual words of a speaker are reproduced in quotes.

Example 1
- Refiloe asked me what time did I return from the movie last night. (*wrong*)
- Refiloe wanted to know at what time I returned from the movie the previous night. (*correct*)

Example 2
- When Thapelo knocked on the door at midnight, her father asked what was the time. (*wrong*)
- When Thapelo knocked on the door at midnight, her father asked her what time it was. (*correct*)

Example 3
- Franz Ramaoka asked how many pupils are involved in the ghastly car accident. (*wrong*)
- Franz Ramaoka wanted to know how many pupils were involved in the ghastly car accident. (*correct*)

It is noteworthy that the verb in the present tense <u>are</u> in sentence 1 is rendered in the past tense <u>were</u> in sentence 2. This rule is applicable in all instances involving reported speech.

Example 4
- Mafumo asked Morongwa when will they get married. (*wrong*)
- Mafumo asked Morongwa when they <u>would</u> get married. (*correct*)

The auxiliary <u>will</u> becomes <u>would</u> in reported speech. In the same vein, <u>shall</u> becomes <u>should</u>, and <u>can</u> becomes <u>could</u>.

Example 5
- Machaba asked Mboweni <u>is</u> it true that the earth rotates on its axis and revolves round the sun? (*wrong*)
- Machaba asked Mboweni if it <u>was</u> true that the earth rotated on its axis and revolved round the sun. (*correct*)

Notice the variation in tenses in sentence 1 and sentence 2 above. This is the way it works in reported speech.

It is worth stressing that grappling with interrogation in reported speech is generally not a piece of cake for people who are non-native speakers of English. The onus is on you to devote ample time to the mastery of this aspect of English grammar.

EXERCISE 1
Put the following dialogue in reported (indirect) speech.
"Do you like Tom?" "Yes."
"Does Rex live here?" "No."
"Have you met Keith before?" "No."
"Will you marry me?" "Yes, I will."

EXERCISE 2
Rewrite the following passage in reported (indirect) speech, beginning with: The president said that . . .

I am very glad to tell you that the asbestos company has made remarkable success in the course of last year. Sales and production have risen dramatically from a record low the previous year.

Our plants have undergone thorough overhaul. In the coming years we hope to buy new machines in order to boost our productivity. We trust that our customers would appreciate this.

EXERCISE 3
Rewrite the following sentences in direct speech.
a) Paul wanted to know if Paulette would like a cup of tea.

b) She asked if I liked going to the movie.
c) They wondered if the pupils had written a test.
d) My father ordered me to shut the door.
e) Hilda said I must not stare at her.
f) Napoleon said that I ought to stop worrying.
g) Pastor Cosmas wanted to know where his keys were.
h) Janet asked what the time was.
i) Albertina would have liked to know where Rina lived.
j) Tomboya wished to know what I was busy at.

Chapter 29

Subjective and Objective Cases

In this lesson, we shall pinpoint a couple of errors that arise from the wrong use of the <u>subjective</u> and <u>objective</u> cases in the English language. Words acting as the subject of a verb are said to be in the <u>subjective case</u> (<u>nominative case</u>).

- <u>Miles and miles of sand</u> attracted the holiday makers.
- <u>A light fall of snow</u> remained from the previous night.

The underlined groups of words in the examples above are in the subjective (nominative) case because they perform the <u>action</u> or <u>state of being</u> denoted in the verb.

Contrarily, any word or group of words that receives or suffers the action described in a verb is said to be in the objective (accusative) case.

- Fire destroyed <u>the office</u>.
- We found a <u>few empty bottles</u>.

The underlined words in the sentences above are in the objective (accusative) case. Quite a few users of English find it rather difficult to handle pronouns in the nominative and accusative cases.

Example 1
- <u>Me</u> and my sisters grew up in this village. (*wrong*)
- My sisters and I grew up in this village. (*correct*)

Example 2
- The journalist interviewed my wife and <u>I</u>. (*wrong*)
- The journalist interviewed my wife and <u>me</u>. (*correct*)

Example 3
- It was <u>him</u> who phoned us at midnight. (*wrong*)
- It was <u>he</u> who phoned us at midnight. (*correct*)

Example 4
- The man <u>who</u> you invited to your wedding is absent. (*wrong*)
- The man <u>whom</u> you invited to your wedding is absent. (*correct*)

Example 5
- The grade 8 pupils played better than <u>them</u>. (*wrong*)

- The grade 8 pupils played better than <u>they</u>. (*correct*) Notice that the sentence above, if extended, would read as follows: the grade 8 pupils played better than <u>they</u> did.

In this lesson I wish to shed some light on errors that speakers of English commit because of poor understanding of the <u>objective</u> and <u>nominative</u> cases in the English language.

Example 1
- My younger brother is taller than <u>me</u>. (*wrong*)
- My younger brother is taller than <u>I</u>. (*correct*)

The word "than" is a conjunction, and can only be followed by a pronoun in the nominative case. The verb that comes after the pronoun is generally omitted.

- My younger brother is taller than I = My younger brother is taller than I (am).

Example 2
- It's <u>him</u> that was seen raping the pupil. (*wrong*)
- It's <u>he</u> that was seen raping the pupil. (*correct*)

The pronoun that comes after the verb <u>to be</u> must be in the <u>nominative case</u>, and not the <u>objective case</u> as seen in the first sentence.

Example 3
- There's no point in <u>me</u> inviting him to the party tonight. (*wrong*)
- There's no point in <u>my</u> inviting him to the party tonight. (*correct*)

When a word ending in -ing is used as a gerund, any noun or pronoun that comes before it must be used in the <u>possessive</u> case as seen in the second sentence above.

Example 4
- There is no misunderstanding between <u>you and I</u>. (*wrong*)
- There is no misunderstanding between <u>you and me</u>. (*correct*)

All prepositions take the objective case. The word <u>between</u> is a preposition and should take the objective <u>me</u> as seen in the second sentence above.

Example 5
- A friend of <u>him</u> told us the bad news. (*wrong*)
- A friend of <u>his</u> told us the bad news. (*correct*)

The <u>double possessive</u> (of + mine, yours, his, etc.) is used when a speaker wishes to emphasize the person who possesses rather than the thing that is possessed.

The proper use of cases is quite challenging, especially for English second language speakers. Teachers should devote ample time to it.

EXERCISE 1
Correct the following sentences.
a) Noah is one of the men who was chosen.
b) Here is one of the cars that was stolen.
c) This green box is one of the boxes that is empty.
d) Vincent is the chap whom broke into my house.
e) Barry and me went to the beach last weekend.
f) Them and I will visit the game reserve next month.
g) It's us who ran the marathon a couple of months ago.
h) It's me who drank your coffee.
i) It is not them who killed the thief.
j) It was her who won the beauty contest.

EXERCISE 2
Rewrite the following wrong sentences correctly.
a) The car belongs to my brother and myself.
b) I and you can tow the car away.
c) To who does this book belong?
d) She is a writer who many people enjoy reading.
e) The man to who you have to complain is Marcela.
f) Fourie is the candidate who you ought to vote for.
g) Stacey is the one whom I think saw what happened.
h) They nominated someone whom they believe was responsible enough to do the job.
i) There is some uncertainty about whom should be chosen.
j) Whom else did you meet at the party?

Chapter 30

Subjunctive Mood

In this lesson, focus shall be on the subjunctive mood and its various functions in English grammar. Fowler (1965: 595) defines the subjunctive mood as the 'use of a verb-form different from the indicative mood in order to denote an action or a state as conceived and not as a fact, and expressing a wish, command, exhortation, or a contingent, hypothetical or prospective event.' We shall use simple examples to show what all this means.

Example 1
- If he <u>was</u> here now he should know what to do. (*wrong*)
- If he <u>were</u> here now he should know what to do. (*correct*) The first sentence is wrong because the speaker has used a wrong tense in the "if clause" - 'if he was here now.' Note that the speaker is expressing a hypothesis that is not a fact. That is why the use of the verb 'were' is justifiable.

Example 2
- During his stay in South Africa, the Crown Prince insisted that President Mandela <u>releases</u> all political prisoners. (*wrong*)
- During his stay in South Africa, the Crown Prince insisted that President Mandela <u>release</u> all political prisoners. (*correct*)

Notice that the first sentence is wrong because the speaker has used the <u>indicative tense</u> 'releases' whereas the <u>subjunctive</u> is desirable because it is an exhortation from the Crown Prince.

Subjunctive Mood

Example 3 He asks that workers' rights <u>are</u> respected. (*wrong*)
- He asks that workers' rights <u>be</u> respected (*correct*). **OR**
- He asks that workers' rights <u>should be</u> respected. (*correct*) The use of the modal auxiliary 'be' as seen in the sentence above has become an established idiom. It is now used after words of <u>command</u> or <u>desire</u> as observed in the example above.

Example 4
- Public opinion demands that elections <u>are</u> free and fair. (*wrong*)

- Public opinion demands that elections <u>be</u> free and fair. (*wrong*)

OR

- Public opinion demands that elections <u>should be</u> free and fair. (*correct*)

As in example 3, this is a desire or wish: the electorate would like to be treated to a free and fair election. This justifies the use of 'to be' in the subjunctive mood.

Example 5

- If I <u>have</u> enough money, I would buy an aeroplane. (*wrong*)
- If I <u>had</u> enough money, I would buy an aeroplane. (*correct*)

Note that the verb 'were' is used for all persons in the 'if clause' to suggest intention as implied in the second sentence.

Example 6

- If you <u>were</u> there yesterday, I should have been happy. (*wrong*)
- If you <u>had been</u> there yesterday, I should have been happy. (*correct*)

Note the concord between the participles: <u>had been</u> and <u>have been</u> in the main and subordinate clauses.

Example 7

- If I <u>was</u> to drop a bomb on the city of Pietersburg tonight, what would you do? (*wrong*)
- If I <u>were</u> to drop a bomb on the city of Pietersburg tonight, what would you do? (*correct*)

Contrary to public opinion, the use of the subjunctive tense is not 'dying.' Subjunctives still form part of our natural speech and occur frequently in conversation as other ways of saying what could have been expressed otherwise.

The literal meaning of subjunctive is dependent or subjoined. In modern English, we use the subjunctive to make a distinction between the world of supposition and the world of fact. In other words, the subjunctive tense helps to show whether we are referring to a fact or to a fantasy. Speakers still use the subjunctive after <u>if</u> where the <u>if-clause</u> expresses a state of things that cannot be real. Do the following exercise for a better understanding of what has been discussed above.

EXERCISE

Put the following sentences in the subjunctive mood.

a) If I was you I would decline the offer.

b) If my father was here he would know what to do in the present circumstances.

c) If he was king he would marry many wives.

d) I wish my mother was here now to alleviate my suffering.

In (e) and (f) the speaker has used the subjunctive tense incorrectly. Rewrite the sentences correctly.

e) That would depend on whether she be convinced or not.

f) It were pointless to try to persuade them.

Chapter 31

Synonyms

When you listen to English second language speakers, it is self-evident that most of them are still grappling with the problem of near-synonymy. Synonyms are words similar in meaning.

Example: abundant/plentiful; aid/help; ally/friend; comprehend/understand; elude/escape and so on. In this lesson, I will revisit some of the frequently confused words in English.

Example 1
- When I entered Mrs. Naidoo's bedroom, I found her on the ground stone dead. (*wrong*)
- When I entered Mrs. Naidoo's bedroom, I found her on the floor stone dead. (*correct*)

In English, floor and ground are carefully distinguished. The floor is the part of the house on which we walk; the ground is outside the house. Care must be taken to avoid the confusion in sentence 1 above.

Example 2
- I would like to know the cost of this gold watch. (*wrong*)
- I would like to know the price of this gold watch. (*correct*)

Once again, cost and price cannot be used interchangeably. Cost is the amount paid by the shopkeeper on an article or commodity. Price is the amount of money paid by the customer. But we can say how much does this gold watch cost?

Example 3
- Mr. Maredi took his woman along on a trip to the Kruger National Park. (*wrong*)
- Mr. Maredi took his wife along on a trip to the Kruger National Park. (*correct*)

In English, woman and wife are clearly distinguished. Woman should not be used instead of wife.

Example 4
- The Grade Nine pupils are staging a theatre tonight titled KE BONA BOLOI. (*wrong*)

- The Grade Nine pupils are staging a <u>play</u> tonight titled KE BONA BOLOI. (*correct*)

A <u>theatre</u> is a building with a stage in it, on which plays, shows and other performances take place. A theatre is not the <u>play</u> itself. Notice that you may substitute <u>drama</u> for <u>play</u>.

Example 5
- The majority of students that I teach have no <u>appetite</u> at all to learn. (*wrong*)
- The majority of students that I teach have no <u>desire</u> at all to learn. (*correct*)

<u>Appetite</u> is generally used for food. For learning, study, work or play, it is desirable to use words like <u>desire</u>, <u>inclination</u> and <u>disposition</u>.

Some speakers of English have cultivated the habit of 'spicing' their language with grandiloquent (big) words in the mistaken belief that high-flown vocabulary is the hallmark of erudition (great knowledge). This is simply not true. This sort of language confuses people. Confucius points out that if what is said is not what is meant; then what ought be done remains undone. Proper words in the proper places is a mark of good style. In this lesson, we shall be discussing a couple of errors that stem from such abusive use of words in the English language.

Example 1
- This old woman is suffering from <u>cecity</u>. (*unfamiliar*)
- This old woman is <u>blind</u>. (*familiar*)

Example 2
- Melanie's grandfather is an <u>octogenarian</u>. (*unfamiliar*)
- Melanie's grandfather is <u>aged between eighty and eighty-nine</u>. (*familiar*)

Example 3
- Pedro, what is the time by your <u>chronometer</u>? (*unfamiliar*)
- Pedro, what is the time by your <u>watch</u>? (*familiar*)   **OR**
- Pedro, what time is it by your <u>watch</u>? (*familiar*)

Example 4
- <u>Cupidity</u> is the main cause of crime in our society. (*unfamiliar*)
- <u>Greed</u> is the main cause of crime in our society. (*familiar*)

Example 5

- He was incarcerated for pilfering. (*unfamiliar*)
- He was imprisoned for stealing. (*familiar*)

Example 6
- Most women spend time confabulating. (*unfamiliar*)
- Most women spend time gossiping. (*familiar*)

The exercises below are intended to help people who are interested in word games. They would provide some mental recreation. It should be noted that it is generally better to use a smaller rather a big word in spoken and written communication.

EXERCISE 1
Supply small words for the following big words.

a) cecity
b) pugilist
c) succinct
d) eschew
e) mendicant
f) impeccable
g) felicitation
h) coerce
i) myriad
j) vanquish
k) chronometer
l) querulous
m) replete
n) rapacious
o) gigantic
p) indolent
q) animosity
r) colossal
s) amity
t) spurious

EXERCISE 2

This exercise deals with lexical comparisons (similes). Fill in the blank spaces in the expressions below.

a) As angry as a___.
b) As blind as a___.
c) As blue as_____.
d) As big as an___.
e) As ancient as___.
f) As brave as_____.
g) As cheerless as a_____.
h) As clear as_____.
i) As docile as a___.
j) As deceitful as a_____.
k) As dark as a___.
l) As cunning as a_____.

m) As countless as_.
n) As complacent as a____.
o) As contrary as_.
p) As devoted as a_____.
q) As eager as a__.
r) As friendly as a_.
s) As glad as a___.
t) As gloomy as__.

Chapter 32

Tautology

In this lesson, we shall focus attention on yet another troublesome aspect of the English language: <u>tautology</u>. Grammarians use this term to refer to a communication situation where a speaker uses many words which have the same meaning in a sentence. Given that in language any redundant word is unacceptable; such a sentence would be incorrect.

The following examples would shed some light on this point:
- The late Kwaito music star was <u>aged</u> twenty-seven years <u>old</u>. (*wrong*)
- The late Kwaito music star was aged twenty-seven. (*correct*)

The first sentence is incorrect because the speaker has used the words <u>aged</u> and <u>old</u> which both refer to the musician's <u>age</u>. Note that it is correct to say: <u>The late Kwaito music star was twenty-seven years old</u>. In this case, you drop the word <u>aged</u>.

- The premier <u>dwelled lengthily</u> on the need to fight crime in the province. (*wrong*)
- The premier dwelled on the need to fight crime in the province. (*correct*)

The first sentence is incorrect because the word <u>dwelled</u> conveys the idea of <u>talked at length about</u>.

Notice that it is correct to say: The premier talked at length about the need to fight crime in the province.

- <u>Please, kindly</u> inform my wife that I left for Pretoria at noon. (*wrong*)
- Please, inform my wife that I left for Pretoria at noon. (*correct*)

The first sentence is incorrect because the speaker has used <u>please</u> and <u>kindly</u> which both convey the idea of <u>politely asking or inviting someone to do something for you</u>.

Notice that it is correct to say: Kindly inform my wife that I left for Pretoria at noon.

- I used my compass to draw a <u>round circle</u> in my workbook. (*wrong*)

- I used my compass to draw a circle in my workbook. (*correct*)

In the first sentence, the word <u>round</u> is redundant because there are no square or rectangular circles. A <u>circle</u> is always <u>round</u>.

Speakers of English would do well to think before speaking because errors of redundancy quite often stem from rapid speech.

In this lesson, we shall revisit the problem of tautology (i.e. unwarranted repetitions) in the English language. Tautological expression is a common error in pupils' essays, letters (formal & informal), reports and other forms of conventional writing.

Examples:
- Your working conditions are <u>more better</u> than mine. (*wrong*)
- Your working conditions are <u>better</u> than mine. (*correct*) The first sentence is wrong because the speaker has used two comparatives <u>more</u> and <u>better</u>. This is grammatically unacceptable.
- Your lifestyle is <u>more preferable</u> to mine. (*wrong*)
- Your lifestyle is preferable to mine. (*correct*)

The first sentence is incorrect because, once again, the speaker has used two comparatives <u>more</u> and <u>preferable</u>. Notice that the word <u>preferable</u> embodies the idea of comparison. This makes the word <u>more</u> redundant in the sentence. It is necessary to emphasise that the word <u>preferable</u> is always followed by the preposition <u>to</u>, and not <u>than</u>. <u>Preferable than</u> is incorrect English usage.

- Please <u>repeat</u> that again, I didn't quite catch it. (*wrong*)
- Please repeat that, I didn't quite catch it. (*correct*)

The first sentence is wrong because the use of <u>repeat</u> and <u>again</u> in the same sentence is tautological. <u>Repeat</u> means <u>say it again</u>.

- I am confident that Dr. Moloto <u>can be able</u> to treat you. (*wrong*)
- I am confident that Dr. Moloto can treat you. (*correct*) Many grammarians would consider the first sentence incorrect because the word <u>can</u> incorporates the idea of <u>to be able to do something</u>. Notice that it is acceptable to say: I am confident that Dr. Moloto would be able to treat you.

Users of English should always be conscious of what they say and write in order to minimise errors of redundancy.

In this lesson, I would like to draw the attention of users of English to some cases of tautology that may make conversational and written English unclear. Tautology obscures meaning. Our newspapers and electronic media are fraught with such errors.

Example 1
- For those <u>unemployed</u> people who are <u>out of work</u>, the government is offering help. (*wrong*)
- The government is offering help to unemployed people. (*correct*) **OR**
- The government is offering help to those people who are out of work. (*correct*)

The first sentence is tautological because <u>unemployed</u> and <u>out of work</u> both refer to <u>jobless</u> persons.

Example 2
- <u>Right now at this moment</u>, a boring TV show is being advertised as a <u>new innovation</u> in the art of the mini-series. (*wrong*)
- <u>Right now</u> a boring TV show is being advertised as an innovation in the art of the mini-series. (*correct*) **OR**
- <u>At this moment</u>, a boring TV show is being advertised as an innovation in the art of the mini-series. (*correct*) **OR**
- <u>At this moment</u>, a boring TV show is being advertised as something new in the art of the mini-series. (*correct*)

It is noteworthy that <u>right now</u> and <u>at this moment</u> are synonymous. By the same token, <u>new and innovation</u> are tautological in the first sentence above.

Example 3
- Let us give <u>grateful thanks</u> that this bachelor is being married to this lovely girl. (*wrong*)
- Let us give <u>thanks</u> that this bachelor is being married to this lovely girl. (*correct*) **OR**
- Let us be <u>grateful</u> that this bachelor is being married to this lovely girl. (*correct*)

<u>Grateful</u> and <u>thanks</u> convey the same idea (i.e being thankful).

Example 4
- The lecture hall was <u>fully filled to capacity</u> on Monday morning. (*wrong*)
- The lecture hall was <u>full</u> on Monday morning. (*correct*) **OR**
- The lecture hall was <u>filled to capacity</u> on Monday morning. (*correct*)

Full and filled to capacity convey the same idea (i.e. completely full).

Example 5
- All our prices have been reduced and customers are requested to come in for free gifts. (*wrong*)
- All our prices have been reduced and customers are requested to come in for gifts. (*correct*)

Free and gift communicate the same notion (i.e. offer).

Example 6
- This project involves both teenagers as well as adults. (*wrong*)
- This project involves teenagers and adults. (*correct*) **OR**
- This project involves both teenagers and adults. (*correct*) The first sentence is tautological because both and as well as are coordinating conjunctions that you use in reference, to two people or things.

Example 7
- I will kill you until you die. (*wrong*)
- I will kill you. (*correct*)

Notice that the first sentence sounds tautological because the word kill incorporates the idea of death. Kill means cause a person, animal or other living thing to die.

Example 8
- I find it hard to walk on foot to my office everyday. (*wrong*)
- I find it hard to walk to my office everyday. (*correct*) **OR**
- I find it hard to go to my office on foot everyday. (*correct*)

Notice that the expression 'on foot' in the first sentence is redundant because walk means move on foot or go on foot.

Example 9
- You have done a very perfect job. (*wrong*)
- You have done a perfect job. (*correct*)

Note that the first sentence is wrong because words like perfect, excellent, unique, etc. suggest the highest degree of a given quality. Thus, it is unnecessary to have them preceded by very.

Example 10
- I am not satisfied with your homework, you will have to redo it again. (*wrong*)

- I am not satisfied with your homework, you will have to do it again. (*correct*)

Note that the first sentence is tautological because <u>redo</u> embodies the idea of <u>do again</u>.

Example 11
- Keep quiet, you <u>dull moron</u>! (*wrong*)
- Keep quiet, you moron! (*correct*) **OR**
- Keep quiet you dull fellow! (*correct*)

Users of English must realise that in attempting to lay stress on a particular idea or quality, they fall into the trap of redundancy. The first sentence is incorrect because a <u>moron</u> is a very dull or <u>stupid</u> person. This is a common mistake in English. Speakers should think before speaking in order to avoid gaffes of this nature.

EXERCISE 1
The following sentences contain some pointless repetitions. Correct them.

a) We advocate placing girls on the same equality with boys.

b) The company's activities are not only limited to paper production.

c) Hard work and hard work alone is the only thing that counts.

d) Muma is equally as clever as Jeanne.

e) Terre Blanche fell off of his horse.

f) The reason why he lied is because he was scared.

g) We met in Kempton Park long since ago.

h) You are nearer Joseph's age than what your sister is.

i) It is imperative that we cooperate together to fight the AIDS pandemic.

j) The minister has returned back to Pretoria after attending the conference in Durban.

EXERCISE 2
Identify the tautologies in the following sentences and rewrite each sentence correctly.

a) Our forward progress was delayed when Dreyer reversed the car backwards.

b) Let's join together and give grateful thanks that this male bachelor is now being married and wedded to this lovely feminine girl.

c) This hall is fully filled to capacity because the film now on is known internationally around the world.

d) Advertisement: Just circle once around the block on our new novelty skateboard and we are sure you will want to repeat the experience again.

e) Advertisement: Our new product kills flies and ants dead and yet it contains no toxic poison.

f) Advertisement: All our prices have been reduced down today so come in and receive a free gift at the door.

g) For those unemployed people who are of out work, the government is offering help.

h) Right now at this moment, a tediously boring TV show is being advertised as a wonderfully new innovation in the art of the mini-series.

Chapter 33

Tenses

English second language users tend to confuse certain words. The following examples would shed some light on this.

Example 1
- I did <u>lent</u> him some money when he was about to get married. (*wrong*)
- I did <u>lend</u> him some money when he was about to get married. (*correct*)

The use of the verb <u>lent</u> after the modal auxiliary <u>did</u> is unacceptable. When <u>did</u> is used for purposes of emphasis, the verb that follows must be in the <u>present tense</u> (e.g. <u>did come</u>, <u>did go</u>, <u>did run</u>, etc.).

Example 2
- I <u>use</u> to smoke like a chimney until lately. (*wrong*)
- I <u>used</u> to smoke like a chimney until lately. (*correct*)

You use the word <u>use</u> in the past tense in combination with the preposition <u>to</u> in order to describe or refer to an action that was done regularly in the past.

Example 3
- Some teachers have served jail terms because they pregnanted pupils. (*wrong*)
- Some teachers have served jail terms for impregnating pupils. (*correct*)

The word <u>pregnanted</u> is an illiteracy. The verb derived from the adjective <u>pregnant</u> is <u>impregnate</u>.

Example 4
- Every evening Mosima <u>is going</u> for a walk. (wrong)
- Every evening Mosima <u>goes</u> for a walk. (*correct*)

The simple <u>present tense</u> (and not the present <u>continuous tense</u>) should be used to express habitual actions implied in the sentence above. But the <u>present continuous</u> tense may express a habitual action when used with the word <u>always</u>. Example: Mosima is <u>always fighting</u> in class.

Example 5
- Last year Mashao <u>was walking</u> to school everyday. (*wrong*)
- Last year Mashao <u>walked</u> to school everyday. (*correct*)

A habitual action in the past is <u>expressed</u> by using the <u>simple past tense</u>, not the <u>past continuous tense</u> as seen in the example above.

Example 6
- We shall phone you when we <u>shall come</u> back. (*wrong*)
- We shall phone you when we <u>come</u> back. (*correct*)

The verb in the <u>time clause</u> must be in the <u>present tense</u> if the verb in the <u>principal clause</u> is in the future tense.

Example 7
- If Duba <u>will ask</u> me, I shall marry him. (*wrong*)
- If Duba <u>asks</u> me I shall marry him. (*correct*)

If the verb in the <u>principal clause</u> is in the <u>future tense</u>, the verb in the <u>time clause</u> must be in the <u>present tense</u> as seen in the second sentence above.

Example 8
- Masingita talks as if she <u>knows</u> everything. (*wrong*)
- Masingita talks as if she <u>knew</u> everything. (*correct*)

<u>As if</u> and <u>as though</u> are phrases that are generally followed by the <u>past tense</u>. Masingita talks as if she knew everything means Masingita talks as <u>she would talk</u> if she knew everything.

The wrong use of tenses is a recurrent problem in the speech of non-native speakers of English. English language teachers would do well to devote enough time to this section of the syllabus.

In this lesson, we shall dwell on the <u>past</u> and <u>past participle</u> tenses of some troublesome verbs in English. It should be noted that certain verbs remain invariable (i.e. unchanged) in the simple past and past participle tenses. These include, among others, <u>broadcast</u>, <u>cast</u>, <u>split</u>, <u>spread</u>, <u>cut</u>, <u>put</u> and <u>cost</u>.

A few examples with the above-mentioned verbs would shed some light on this lesson.

Example 1
- News of Sifiso Nkabinde's gruesome murder was <u>broadcasted</u> on national television and radio. (*wrong*)
- News of Sifiso Nkabinde's gruesome murder was <u>broadcast</u> on national television and radio. (*correct*)

Example 2
- The Deputy President <u>casted</u> his vote at ten o'clock. (*wrong*)
- The Deputy President <u>cast</u> his vote at ten o'clock. (*correct*) The two sentences above would be written in the past participle form as follows:
- News of Sifiso Nkabinde's gruesome murder has <u>been broadcast</u> on national television and radio. (*correct*)
- The Deputy President <u>has cast</u> his vote. (*correct*)

Example 3
- The National Party <u>splitted</u> into two factions. (*wrong*)
- The National Party <u>split</u> into two factions. (*correct*)

Note that this sentence would be written in the past participle form as follows: The National Party <u>has split</u> into two factions. (*correct*)

Example 4
- The bad news <u>spreaded</u> like wildfire through the city. (*wrong*)
- The bad news <u>spread</u> like wildfire through the city. (*correct*) In the past participle form, this sentence would read as follows:
- The bad news <u>has spread</u> like wild fire through the city.

It is noteworthy that if something, especially news or a rumour, spreads like wild fire, it spreads extremely quickly. Example: The stories are spreading like wild fire through the town.

Example 5
- ESKOM has <u>cutted</u> the source of power supply. (*wrong*)
- ESKOM <u>has cut</u> the source of power supply. (*correct*)
- She <u>cutted</u> herself with a kitchen knife. (*wrong*)
- She <u>cut</u> herself with a kitchen knife. (*correct*)

Example 6
- Throughout his career, he <u>has putted</u> the cart before the horse. (*wrong*)
- Throughout his career he <u>has put</u> the cart before the horse. (*correct*)

The idiomatic expression "put the cart before the horse" means do things in the wrong order.

In a nutshell, there are quite a few troublesome verbs in English that harbour communication pitfalls. Speakers of English should acquaint themselves with such verbs.

In this lesson, I would like to draw the attention of readers to frequent errors in written and spoken English associated with the wrong use of the simple past tense in negative sentences. As the name implies, the simple past tense is used when a speaker wishes to say that something happened or took place and was definitely finished or completed in the past.

Example 1
- Chuene and Phukubje went to Pretoria but didn't saw their uncle. (*wrong*)
- Chuene and Phukubje went to Pretoria but didn't see their uncle. (*correct*)

When the auxiliary verb do in the past (i.e. did) precedes a verb, it is appropriate to have that verb in the present tense as seen in the second sentence above.

Example 2
- Masemola didn't played the match because of a knee injury. (*wrong*)
- Masemola didn't play the match because of a knee injury. (*correct*)

The use of the simple past tense played in sentence 1 is unacceptable because didn't indicates past tense.

Example 3
- I did sent the sum of R1000, being hostel and school fees for my daughter, Paulina Mehlape. (*wrong*)
- I did send the sum of R1000, being hostel and school fees for my daughter, Paulina Mehlape. (*correct*)

Notice that after the verb did, it is incorrect to use the past tense sent as seen in sentence 1 above. Did should be followed by the present tense send.

Example 4
- When the hostel master walked into our room, we was all fast asleep. (*wrong*)
- When the hostel master walked into our room, we were all fast asleep. (*correct*)

Notice that there is no concord (agreement) between the past tense was and the subject of the sentence we.

Example 5
- Mabelebele and his fiancée <u>couldn't agreed</u> on the brand of car to buy for their wedding. (*wrong*)
- Mabelebele and his fiancée <u>couldn't agree</u> on the brand of car to buy for their wedding. (*correct*)

Silly mistakes like these can mar conversation and writing. Sometimes they are quite irritating. Others find them even humorous. It is desirable for English second and third language speakers to dedicate enough time to the mastery of tenses in English.

In this lesson, I will be shedding some light on the correct usage of the <u>past continuous tense</u> in English. When we want to convey the fact that two or more actions took place in the past and that one of the actions was interrupted or left unfinished, we express the incomplete action in the <u>past continuous tense</u>. The following examples will clarify the point.

Example 1
- Mokwena <u>jumped off</u> the bus while it <u>moved</u>. (*wrong*)
- Mokwena jumped off the bus while it <u>was moving</u>. (*correct*)

Notice that the verb <u>move</u> is used in the <u>past continuous tense</u> in the second sentence to indicate an <u>incomplete</u> action in the past.

Example 2
- A few moments ago Ramonyai <u>told</u> Dipela to listen because the teacher <u>talked</u> to her. (*wrong*)
- A few moments ago, Ramonyai told Dipela to listen because the teacher <u>was talking</u> to her. (*correct*)

The verb <u>talk</u> is used in the <u>past continuous</u> tense above to express an <u>unfinished</u> action in the past.

Example 3
- I <u>walked</u> home this afternoon when an accident occurred just in front of me. (*wrong*)
- I <u>was walking</u> home this afternoon when an accident <u>occurred</u> just in front of me. (*correct*)

Note the use of <u>walk</u> in the <u>past continuous</u> tense to express an action that was left <u>unfinished</u> in the second sentence above.

Example 4

- As I <u>arrived</u> at the office this morning, the telephone <u>rang</u>. (*wrong*)
- As I <u>arrived</u> at the office this morning, the telephone <u>was ringing</u>. (*correct*)

Notice that <u>was ringing</u> expresses the fact that the ringing of phone was <u>unfinished</u> at the time the speaker arrived at the office.

Example 5

- Sentike said that she did not know who <u>made</u> the noise when I <u>complained</u>. (*wrong*)
- Sentike said that she did not know who <u>was making</u> the noise when I <u>complained</u>. (*correct*)

Note that the past continuous tense <u>was making</u> indicates that two actions, namely <u>making a noise</u> and <u>complaining</u> took place at the same time.

Example 6

- Rammutia <u>met</u> his friend as he <u>had left</u> the cinema last night. (*wrong*)
- Rammutia <u>met</u> his friend as he <u>was leaving</u> the cinema last night. (*correct*)

In English, as in other languages, <u>time</u> is <u>relative</u>. There has to be some means of differentiating in time the various thoughts and happenings that humans usually chronicle in words. This is done by a device called <u>tense</u>. It is by the use of the appropriate tense in speech or writing that our readers or listeners can deduce for themselves when the action took place.

In this lesson we shall revisit some problems arising from the confusion of tenses in the English language. Care should be taken to sustain the tense of an original thought right through a sentence. Sometimes, this is difficult in the case of complex sentences where the tense of the verb in the <u>subordinate clause</u> depends on the tense of the verb in the <u>main clause</u>. Let's look at the following examples for clarification.

Example 1

- I asked my mother whether I may go to America this year to begin my studies and she said that I <u>can</u>. (*wrong*)
- I asked my mother whether I might go to America this year to begin my studies and she said that I <u>could</u>. (*correct*)

The tenses in the first sentence are incorrect. The main clauses are: 'I asked my mother' and 'she said.' These clauses are in the simple past tense as evidenced by use of the verbs <u>asked</u> and <u>said</u>. Consequently, the rest of the sentence should be in the simple past tense as seen in the second sentence.

Example 2
- The building which <u>is</u> collapsing, <u>has been</u> demolished. (*wrong*)
- The building which <u>was</u> collapsing <u>has been</u> demolished. (*correct*)

Notice the concord in tense (i.e. past tense) in the main clause and the subordinate adjectival clause 'which was collapsing.'

Example 3
- What they <u>said surprises</u> everyone in the audience. (*wrong*)
- What he <u>said surprised</u> everyone in the audience. (*correct*) <u>Said</u> and <u>surprised</u> are both in the past tense in the second sentence.

Example 4
- He <u>regretted</u> the fact that he <u>loses</u> his temper in the course of the argument. (*wrong*)
- He <u>regretted</u> the fact that he <u>lost</u> his temper in the course of the argument. (*correct*)

There is concord between the verb (regretted) in the main clause and the verb (lost) in the subordinate 'that clause' – <u>that he lost his temper</u> in the second sentence.

Example 5
- She <u>ran</u> so fast that her glasses <u>fall</u> off. (*wrong*)
- She <u>ran</u> so fast that her glasses <u>fell</u> off. (*correct*)

Note the concord between the verb (ran) in the main clause and (fell) in the subordinate adverbial clause -- <u>so fast that her glasses fell off</u>.

Example 6
- Paul <u>slammed</u> the door because he <u>is</u> furious. (*wrong*)
- Paul <u>slammed</u> the door because he <u>was</u> furious. (*correct*)

Notice the concord in tense between <u>slammed</u> in the main clause and <u>was</u> in the subordinate clause.

Example 7
- Timothy <u>played</u> as he <u>has</u> never played before. (*wrong*)

- Timothy <u>played</u> as he <u>had</u> never played before. (*correct*)

The second sentence is acceptable because there is concord in tense between the verb <u>played</u> in the main clause and <u>had played</u> in the subordinate adverbial clause -- <u>as he had never played</u> before.

Tense concord in complex sentences poses quite a few problems. Teachers should devote ample time to the teaching of this aspect of language.

EXERCISE 1

Rewrite the following sentences leaving out <u>WHO</u>, <u>WHICH</u>, and <u>THAT</u> and changing the verb to the present continuous tense.

a) Here is a box which contains several tools.

b) People who live in remote areas seldom come to the city.

c) Daniel bought some provisions which included soap, omo, dishwashing liquid, foam-bath and toilet tissue.

d) There is a five-metre fence that encloses the school.

e) AIDS is a viral disease that affects intravenous drug users.

f) A barrage is a large wall across a river that makes a sort of dam for irrigation.

g) Soil is the thin layer of the ground that consists of tiny particles of rock, rotted plants and some living organisms.

h) Plasma is the clear fluid part of blood which comprises the corpuscles and cells.

i) A pentagon is a figure which has five sides.

j) We saw a man who wore a leopard skin waistcoat.

EXERCISE 2

Put the following sentences in the past tense.

a) Ten o'clock is my father's busiest time.

b) The orphans have to be bathed and fed.

c) The police-men are going to the gangster's home.

d) The rapist was hiding behind the wall at night.

e) A new shop has been opened around the corner.

f) You can buy provisions cheap at this supermarket.

g) Many pedestrians have been killed by drunk drivers.

h) We plan to visit the Zambezi at our earliest convenience.

i) My sister likes winter so much.

j) You need a visa in order to visit Botswana.

EXERCISE 3

Complete these sentences with one of the words in the following list:

sentenced, defended, asked, testified, called, let, pleaded, proved, contradicted, committed.

a) The accused has_____several crimes.
b) They were____to imprisonment.
c) I____not guilty.
d) My aunt was__by a lawyer.
e) Counsel for the defence_____many witnesses.
f) They__under oath that the accused was innocent.
g) One of the offenders__himself when crossed-questioned.
h) The prosecutor insisted that the accused was guilty and ____ for a conviction.
i) The magistrate_the accused off with a warning.
j) The attorney said that it could not be _ beyond reasonable doubt that the accused was guilty.

Chapter 34

Verbs

Verbs are a vital component of the English Language. Sadly enough, not many speakers of English have a firm grasp of this part of speech. Perhaps a discussion of some common errors that stem from the wrong use of modal verbs would be of help.

Modal verbs (modal auxiliaries) are generally found before main verbs. Modals include: <u>will</u>, <u>would</u>, <u>shall</u>, <u>should</u>, <u>can</u>, <u>could</u>, <u>may</u>, <u>might</u>, <u>ought to</u>, <u>have to</u>, etc. The wrong choice of a modal can alter the way a speaker desires to be understood.

Example 1
- I trust that Sesoga <u>shall</u> be back from overseas before classes begin. (*wrong*)
- I trust that Sesoga <u>will</u> be back from overseas before classes begin. (*correct*)

<u>Shall</u> expresses insistence on the part of a speaker. Conversely, <u>will</u> expresses a certain degree of confidence (see <u>I trust</u>) in sentence 2 above.

Example 2
- We hope Seema <u>should</u> pass his examination this year. (*wrong*)
- We hope Seema <u>will</u> pass his examination this year. (*correct*)

Generally, <u>should</u> expresses <u>obligation</u> or <u>necessity</u>. It is correct to say: We said <u>Seema</u> should do everything possible to pass his examination this year.

Example 3
- <u>Might</u> be the people's poet was involved in the bank robbery. (*wrong*)
- <u>Maybe</u> the people's poet was involved in the bank robbery. (*correct*)

<u>Maybe</u> is used to express uncertainty, especially when you aren't sure that something is definitely true. You also use <u>maybe</u> when you are making a rough guess at a number, quantity or value. Example: The house is situated maybe a hundred kilometres away. On the other

hand, you use <u>might</u> to make a suggestion or give advice in a very polite way.

In this lesson, we shall examine common mistakes in written and spoken English associated with another category of verbs (i.e. <u>stative</u> verbs). Stative verbs express a condition or state of being. They are not action words. Examples include: <u>have</u>, <u>be</u>, <u>know</u>, <u>belong</u>, etc. Students often fall into the trap of giving stative verbs continuous forms as seen in the examples below.

Example 1
- This business economics book <u>is belonging</u> to Tumisho. (*wrong*)
- This business economics book <u>belongs</u> to Tumisho. (*correct*)

<u>Belong</u> is a stative verb and shouldn't be given a continuous form as seen in sentence 1 above.

Example 2
- I <u>am having</u> two assignments to do before lessons begin tomorrow. (*wrong*)
- I <u>have</u> two assignments to do before lessons begin tomorrow. (*correct*)

<u>To have</u> is a stative verb. Consequently, instead of giving it a <u>present continuous</u> form (see sentence 1), it is correct to use the <u>present simple</u> tense (see sentence 2).

Example 3
- Mashao <u>is finding</u> it hard to believe Movalo's weird story. (*wrong*)
- Mashao <u>finds</u> it hard to believe Movalo's weird story. (*correct*)

There is no justification for using the verb <u>find</u> in the present continuous form as seen in sentence 1 above. The present simple tense should be used (see sentence 2).

Example 4
- I <u>am seeing</u> vapour rising from the sea. (*wrong*)
- I <u>can see</u> vapour rising from the sea. (*correct*)

<u>See</u> is a member of the stative group of verbs, which generally have no continuous form.

Example 5
- I <u>am knowing</u> that you're my best friend and will never let me down. (*wrong*)

- I <u>know</u> that you're my best friend and will never let me down. (*correct*)

The point to note about <u>stative</u> verbs is that they <u>do not</u> have continuous tenses. Speakers of English should use the <u>present simple</u> tense instead of the <u>present continuous</u>: and the <u>past simple</u> rather than the <u>past continuous</u> tense.

In this lesson, we shall dwell on the use of auxiliary verbs in the English language. An auxiliary, as the name implies, is a <u>helping</u> word. It is used in combination with the main verb to perform a specific function in the sentence. Auxiliary verbs include: <u>be</u>, <u>have</u>, and <u>do</u>. They play the following functions: form tenses, form negatives, form question tags and ask questions. Quite a few errors made by speakers of English in daily conversation and writing are associated with the use of auxiliaries. Many of these mistakes stem from a poor mastery of the grammatical functions of auxiliaries. We shall use a couple of examples to clarify what has been said above.

Example 1

- My mother would like to know at what time did the plane <u>arrived</u>. (*wrong*)
- My mother would like to know at what time the plane <u>arrived</u>. (*correct*)

The first sentence is incorrect because the speaker has used the main verb 'arrive' in the past tense whereas it should have remained in the present tense.

Example 2

- I am pleased because my students did <u>performed</u> well in the debating tournament. (*wrong*)
- I am pleased because my students did <u>perform</u> well in the debating tournament. (*correct*) **OR**
- I am pleased because my students <u>performed</u> well in the debating tournament. (*correct*)

When the main verb (perform) is in the past tense, it is desirable to drop the auxiliary verb as seen in the alternative sentence above.

Example 3

- The pupils are studying, <u>isn't it</u>? (*wrong*)
- The pupils are studying, <u>aren't they</u>? (*correct*)

The first sentence is incorrect because the speaker has used the wrong question tag (i.e. isn't it?). The <u>question tag</u> usually has the same auxiliary as the verb in the main sentence. In the example above, the auxiliary verb is 'are' (studying). Therefore, the auxiliary in the question tag ought to be '<u>aren't</u>' (they)?

Example 4
- The goods were not sold, <u>weren't they</u>? (*wrong*)
- The goods were not sold, <u>were they</u>? (*correct*)

A <u>negative</u> sentence takes a <u>positive</u> question tag, whereas a <u>positive</u> sentence takes a <u>negative</u> tag. The sentence above is <u>negative</u>. Consequently, the question tag should be <u>positive</u>.

Example 5
- You want to take Molema as wife, isn't it? (*wrong*)
- You want to take Molema as wife, don't you? (*correct*) Notice that the question is <u>positive</u> and elicits a negative question tag.

The use of auxiliary verbs is quite a slippery aspect of the English grammar. English language teachers should lay sufficient stress on this right from the onset (i.e. junior grades).

EXERCISE 1
Supply the correct form of the verbs in brackets in the sentences below.
a) Alan always (tell) the truth.
b) Braam (say) he hates cats.
c) Perold is (say) nothing at the moment.
d) They (think) Mike is ill.
e) Mr. Walker (insist) on leaving next week.
f) I will (ask) Elias to pray for us.
g) He (believe) he will get lost in the forest.
h) What is she (demand)?
i) Joel does not (like) people who tell lies.
j) Elvis (notify) us that he would go on vacation in November.

EXERCISE 2
Combine the verbs in the following sentences with <u>shall</u> or <u>will</u>.
a) Phoku says tomorrow___be his birthday.
b) Denis says, he___come along with us.
c) You___stay in this classroom until your assignment is done.

d) _____ Nformi bring his own car?
e) Fela___go to school next academic year.
f) No! Justina___never marry that man.
g) Jang___write three letters to the bank tomorrow.
h) Ngenge_____do it as a last resort.
i) Tabong___find his books on the table when he arrives.
j) Kima says he__be as quiet as a mouse during the meeting.

Chapter 35

Words Commonly Confused

The focus of this lesson is the mastery of basic rules in grammar, notably rules pertaining to parts of speech, tenses, prepositions, clauses, sentence structure and so on. Such mastery would enable learners to avoid the confusion of words that is rampant in tests, assignments and examination scripts that teachers correct.

Example 1
- I am <u>sorry for</u> what I did to you yesterday. (*wrong*)
- I am <u>sorry about</u> what I did to you yesterday. (*correct*)

Generally, you are <u>sorry about</u> a mistake or an offence you have committed. On the other hand, you are <u>sorry for</u> someone who is unhappy or in an unpleasant situation.

Example 2
- The candidate is <u>accused for</u> cheating in the examination. (*wrong*)
- The candidate is <u>accused of</u> cheating in the examination. (*correct*)

You <u>accuse</u> someone <u>of</u> doing something wrong or dishonest.

Example 3
- I am <u>waiting upon</u> my daughter who said she would be back in a couple of minutes. (*wrong*)
- I am <u>waiting for</u> my daughter who said she would be back in a couple of minutes. (*correct*)

To wait for someone is to stay expecting them to come or do something. Conversely, to wait upon someone is to act as a servant to them or look after them or attend to them.

Example 4
- The granny and her grandson went to the zoo <u>by foot</u>. (*wrong*)
- The granny and her grandson went the zoo <u>on foot</u>. (*correct*)

If you go somewhere <u>on foot</u> you <u>walk</u> rather than use any other form of transport.

Example 5
- The councillor <u>insisted to see</u> the premier. (*wrong*)

- The councillor <u>insisted on seeing</u> the premier. (*correct*) The verb <u>insist</u> is generally followed by the preposition <u>on</u> and another verb in the present continuous tense.

There are many words which speakers of English tend to confuse. A discussion of some of such words may be of help. Words commonly confused include: <u>lend</u> / <u>borrow</u>; <u>live</u> / <u>stay</u>; <u>loads</u> / <u>luggage</u>; <u>work</u> / <u>works</u>; <u>damage</u> / <u>damages</u>.

Example 1

- Would you <u>borrow</u> me your car for my wedding tomorrow? (*wrong*)
- Would you <u>lend</u> me your car for my wedding tomorrow? (*correct*)

When requesting someone to give you something, e.g. car, you should say 'would you lend me your car?' or 'may I borrow your car?'

Example 2

- I <u>stay</u> at No. 85 Paul Kruger Street in Pietersburg. (*wrong*)
- I <u>live</u> at No. 85 Paul Kruger Street in Pietersburg. (*correct*) We use the word <u>stay</u> when we mean only a temporary sojourn. When we want to indicate that this is the address at which we are normally to be found, we use the word <u>live</u>.

Example 3

- I am going to get my <u>loads</u> ready for a trip to Newcastle. (*wrong*)
- I am going to get my <u>luggage</u> ready for a trip to Newcastle. (*correct*)

We never refer to our personal belongings as <u>loads</u>. We use the word luggage, which is a singular word with a plural connotation.

Example 4

- I hear that there are a lot of <u>works</u> at the new textile company. (*wrong*)
- I hear that there is a lot of work at the new textile company. (*correct*) **OR**
- I hear there will be jobs for many people at the new textile company. (*correct*)

<u>Works</u> means a factory or assembly plant where people carry on their job. <u>Works</u> is also used in the sense of a writer's or artist's works.

Example 5
- Mr. Maluleke was vindicated in court last week and <u>damage</u> was paid. (*wrong*)
- Mr. Maluleke was vindicated in court last week and <u>damages</u> <u>were</u> paid. (*correct*)

When the word <u>damage</u> is used in the singular it means destruction of some kind but when it carries an -s, it means legal compensation for some injury suffered. For example, the storm caused a great deal of <u>damage</u> to the houses / The court awarded Mr. Rammutia R5000 in <u>damages</u>.

In this lesson, I would like to discuss more words that are frequently confused by speakers of English. In quite a few cases the problem stems from the fact that the words are near-homonyms (i.e. words spelt and pronounced in almost the same way but having different meanings).

Example 1
- This sportsman is <u>elder</u> than that one. (*wrong*)
- This sportsman is <u>older</u> than that one. (*correct*)

<u>Older</u> and <u>oldest</u> apply to persons and things, whereas <u>elder</u> and <u>eldest</u> are used in relation to persons. <u>Elder</u> and <u>eldest</u> cannot be followed by the comparative <u>than</u> as seen in the example above.

Example 2
- I am not <u>interesting</u> in the job you have offered me. (*wrong*)
- I am not <u>interested</u> in the job you have offered me. (*correct*)

<u>Interesting</u> refers to the thing which arouses interest, while <u>interested</u> is used in reference to the person who takes an interest in the thing mentioned, (e.g. job in the example above).

Example 3
- She returned home <u>latter</u> than I. (*wrong*)
- She returned home <u>later</u> than I. (*correct*)

<u>Later</u> refers to time. <u>Latter</u> applies to order and means the second of two things just mentioned. For instance, Soweto and Alexandra are townships, the <u>latter</u> has a population of over a million.

Example 4
- Lebo has <u>less</u> books than Leko. (*wrong*)
- Lebo has <u>fewer</u> books than Leko. (*correct*)

Less denotes amount, quantity, value or degree. On the other hand, fewer refers to number. Thus, we may have less water, less food, less money, less education, but fewer books, fewer clothes, fewer friends.

Example 5
- My teacher is ten feet high. (*wrong*)
- My teacher is ten feet tall. (*correct*)

Tall is generally used for persons, and is the opposite of short. High is used in relation to buildings, trees or mountains and is the opposite of low.

Example 6
- Maila picked one ring in the street on her way from school. (*wrong*)
- Maila picked a ring in the street on her way from school. (*correct*)

The numeral "one" should not be used instead of the indefinite article "a" or "an" as the speaker has done in sentence 1 above. It is advisable to use "one" only where the number is emphatic, for example, Maila gave me one ring instead of two.

Example 7
- I haven't some assignments to do, so I'm going to the movie. (*wrong*)
- I haven't any assignments to do, so I'm going to the movie. (*correct*)

"Any" not "some" should be used in negative sentences as seen above. "Some" is generally used in affirmative sentences expecting an affirmative answer. Example: Will you bring me some wine?

Example 8
- Aluwani paid me a visit in the later part of the evening. (*wrong*)
- Aluwani paid me a visit in the latter part of the evening. (*correct*)

"Later" and "latter" are not synonyms. "Later" refers to a time after the present one. Example: I'll join you later. "Latter" is used to describe the later part of a period of time. Example: He is getting into the latter years of his career.

Example 9
- Mabasa is three years bigger than Pheedi. (*wrong*)

- Mabasa is three years older than Pheedi. (*correct*)

If reference is being made to <u>age</u>, it is desirable to use "young" or "old." "Big" and "small" usually refer to <u>size</u>.

Example 10
- Letsoalo told me an interesting <u>history</u> about her grandfather. (*wrong*)
- Letsoalo told me an interesting <u>story</u> about her grandfather. (*correct*)

Many non-native speakers of English confuse <u>story</u> with <u>history</u>. A <u>story</u> is an account of an event or events that may or may not be true. <u>History</u> is a systematic record of past events.

Every effort should be made to avoid malapropisms of this nature.

Many English second language speakers frequently fall into the trap of confusing words such as: <u>died/dead</u>; <u>shoot/shot</u>; <u>its/it's</u>; <u>well/good</u>; <u>weighted/weighed</u>; <u>fool/foolish</u> and so on.

Example 1
- Nicola broke the news that his grandfather is <u>died</u>. (*wrong*)
- Nicola broke the news that his grandfather was <u>dead</u>. (*correct*)

<u>Died</u> and <u>dead</u> cannot be used interchangeably. <u>Died</u> is the past tense of <u>die</u>. The adjective is <u>dead</u>.

Example 2
- Pollen Ndlanya made a good <u>shoot</u> at the goal. (*wrong*)
- Pollen Ndlanya made a good <u>shot</u> at the goal. (*correct*) In soccer terminology, <u>shoot</u> is the verb, the noun is <u>shot</u>.

Example 3
- When the hunter fired a shot, the lioness ran away leaving <u>it's</u> cubs to their own devices. (*wrong*)
- When the hunter fired a shot, the lioness ran away leaving <u>its</u> cubs to their own devices. (*correct*)

The possessive adjective <u>its</u> is written without an apostrophe. <u>It's</u> is a contraction of <u>it is</u>.

Example 4
- My teacher always says I am a <u>foolish</u>. (*wrong*)
- My teacher always says I am foolish. (*correct*) **OR**
- My teacher always says I am a <u>fool</u>. (*correct*)

Fool is a noun, and requires an article when used with the verb to be. Foolish is an adjective, and cannot be used with an article as seen sentence 1 above.

Example 5
- Mohamed Auseb plays soccer very good. (*wrong*)
- Mohamed Auseb plays soccer very well. (*correct*)

Good is an adjective, and cannot be used as an adverb as the speaker has done in sentence 1 above. This error is attributable to the speaker's insufficient mastery of the various parts of speech in English.

Example 6
- Have you weighted the luggage destined for Johannesburg? (*wrong*)
- Have you weighed the luggage destined for Johannesburg? (*correct*)

Weight is a noun and cannot be used as a verb. The verb is weigh (without the 't').

Other frequently confused words include: deny/refuse, credit/debit, borrow/lend, convince/persuade, hire/let, revenge/avenge, etc. A couple of examples would shed some light on the use of these words.

Example 1
- Please ask Tina to borrow me her car. (*wrong*)
- Please, ask Tina to lend me her car. (*correct*)

Notice that the person who 'lends' something allows someone to have or use it for a period of time. On the other hand, the person who 'borrows' something takes and uses it for a fixed period of time.

Example 2
- Nsako has denied to play soccer this afternoon. (*wrong*)
- Nsako has refused to play soccer this afternoon. (*correct*)

Notice that 'deny' means 'answer in the negative or state that something is not true.' On the other hand, 'refuse' means say firmly that you will not do something.

Example 3
- The old man has avenged himself on his attackers. (*wrong*)
- The old man has revenged himself on his attackers. (*correct*)

To 'revenge oneself' on someone who has hurt you means 'to hurt them in return.' Conversely, 'to avenge' a wrong or harmful act means 'to hurt or punish a wrongdoer on behalf of another person.'

Example 4
- The policeman said he was <u>persuaded</u> of my innocence. (*wrong*)
- The policeman said he was <u>convinced</u> of my innocence. (*correct*)

'Persuade' and 'convince' have different contextual meanings. To <u>persuade</u> someone to do something means 'to cause them to do it by giving them good reasons for doing it.' On the contrary, to <u>convince</u> someone of something 'means to make them believe that it is true or that it exists.'

Example 5
- The house in which we live has been <u>hired</u> to us by Mr. Stone. (*wrong*)
- The house in which we live has been <u>let</u> to us by Mr. Stone. (*correct*)

The verb 'hire' is used when you get something (e.g. car, services, etc.) for use in return for payment. Contrarily, to 'let' (e.g. a house, land, etc.) means <u>allow</u> it to be used in exchange for money. Note that the beneficiary 'rents' the house or land.

Example 6
- I am richer today, my account has been <u>debited</u>. (*wrong*)
- I am richer today, my account has been <u>credited</u>. (*correct*)

Notice that when your bank <u>debits</u> your account, money is taken from it and paid to someone else. When your account is <u>credited</u>, some money is added to it.

The words discussed above have very subtle meaning differences that may spring surprises on users of English. It would be rewarding to pay extra attention when using them in all forms of writing.

Chapter 36

Cameroonisms and Camerounismes

In this chapter, we introduce readers to some commonly used Cameroonian English language expressions that may literally shock or baffle the native speaker of English. These expressions are referred to as *cameroonisms* or camerounismes[1] in the French language. We have culled some of our examples from Jean-Paul Kouega's book titled *A Dictionary of Cameroon Pidgin Usage* (2007). Others come from a seminal work on Cameroon Pidgin English (CPE) by Ayafor and Green, titled *Cameroon Pidgin English* (2017). Finally, Hector Kamdem Fonkou's book on Camfanglais titled *A Dictionary of Camfranglais* (2015) came in handy. It is noteworthy that Cameroon is a melting pot of over two hundred indigenous languages, including French and English (languages imposed on Cameroonians by colonialists). This linguistic cacophony has resulted in what may be termed linguistic 'glottophagy', a term used by linguists to describe the absorption or replacement of minor languages or dialects by major ones as readers will see in the examples provided in this chapter.

A

Achu: the staple food of Cameroonians from the North-West Region.

Afofo: a strong alcoholic drink distilled from malted corn.

Akwara: a prostitute/call girl/street-walker.

Amba: Abbreviation of Ambazonia.

Amba boys: reference to the Southern Cameroonian freedom fighters

Ambazonia: Word that refers to British Southern Cameroons.

Anglo: Abbreviation of Anglophone. This term is often used derogatorily by French-speaking Cameroonians to ridicule their English-speaking compatriots.

---

[1] French and English colonization of Cameroon resulted in a sort of bilingualism and biculturalism that have had a significant impact on the way Cameroonians speak both languages.

Anglo-fou: pejorative term used by French-speaking Cameroonians to ridicule their English-speaking compatriots. Literally, it means mad or insane Anglophone.

Ashia: Cameroon Pidgin English term used as a greeting or consolatory expression directed at someone who is in a difficult situation.

Ashuka: Cameroon Pidgin English term used in reference to punishment that the recipient deserves.

Asso: Expression used in reference to a person from whom one buys or sells commodities on a regular basis.

Awuf: something taken free of charge.

B

Bahat: Pidgin English term that describes bitterness, spitefulness or hatred.

Bami: This word is an abbreviation of the word 'Bamileke, one of the ethnic groups in Cameroon.

Bangala: Pidgin English term for penis.

Beans: Pidgin English term for female genitalia.

Beer parlor: term for unlicensed home where food and drinks are sold.

Beleh: Pidgin English word pregnancy.

Bendskin: a motorcycle used for the transportation of passengers.

Beret-Khaki: term of insult used in reference to police-men and police-women. A synonymous term is *mange-mill.*

Biafran: Derogatory term used by French-speaking Cameroonians to describe English-speaking Cameroonians who are advocating for secession from la République du Cameroun. The French equivalent is *biafrais.*

Bita Kola: a type of kola nut eaten by Cameroonians who believe that it is an aphrodisiac.

Bosco: a strongly built man.

Boyses: Term coined by Cameroon's Minister of Territorial Administration, Mr. Atanga Nji. This word refers to the Ambazonian freedom fighters. It bears pointing out that this term does not exist in the English language dictionary.

Bumbu: Pidgin English term for vagina.

Bush: Pidgin English term for forest.

Bush-beef: Pidgin English term for game.

Bush-faller: an immigrant/someone who chooses to leave his native country to go in search of greener pastures.

Bushman: Pidgin English term for an uncivilized individual.

Buyam-sellam: Pidgin English term for man or woman who buys and sells foodstuff.

C

Camer: abbreviation for Cameroon/Cameroun.

Chango: Pidgin English term for men whose wives come from the same family.

Chantier: French language term for place where food, drinks and others eatables can be purchased.

Chei! Pidgin English expression for surprise.

Chicken parlor: term for unlicensed home where food and drinks are sold.

Choko: Pidgin English term for a tip or bribe.

Chop-chair: Pidgin English expression for heir or successor.

Chop die: Pidgin English expression referring to a reckless person.

Circuit: term for unlicensed home where food and drinks are sold.

Clando: term for personal care used illegally as a taxi.

Come no go: term for Cameroonians from other regions living in the Southwest Region.

Come-we-stay: Pidgin English term for officious marriage.

Country-fashion: Pidgin English term used in reference to mystic practices performed by most Cameroonians in a bid to appease the ancestors.

Country man: Pidgin English term used to describe a man who comes from the village as the speaker. It can also mean an uncivilized man.

D

Damba: Pidgin English term used in reference to football/soccer.

Dash: Pidgin English term for a gift.

Death celebration: ceremony organized by relatives of a deceased person in remembrance of him or her. This term is synonymous with *cry-die*.

Deuxième bureau: mistress or concubine.

Dibia: Pidgin English term for a fortune-teller.

Die house: Pidgin English term for the residence of a deceased person where mourners have assembled for wake-keeping.

Djigi-djaga: Pidgin English term for the cuddling and other movements made by lovers they are having sex.

Djim: Pidgin English term for someone or something big or large.

Djim-djim: Pidgin English term for someone big.

E

Ekie! Local language term expressing surprise.

Eleventh Province: Pidgin English term to describe English-speaking Cameroonians who are not by definition natives of the North-West or South-West regions. These are generally Francophones whose parents immigrated to Southern Cameroons during the turbulent years of the decolonization struggle.

Ekwang: Local language term for grated cocoyam wrapped in cocoyam leaves and cooked with various ingredients.

Elobi: Local language term for swamp.

Eru: local vegetable used for cooking traditional dishes.

F

Fall bush: Pidgin English word that describes anyone who leaves his or her native country to seek greener pastures.

Family way: to live with a girl without being legally married.

Famla: witchcraft

Fey: term meaning to, scam, dupe, deceive, trick or swindle.

Feyman: term for crook, dealer, conman, scammer or swindler.

Feywoman: term for crook, dealer, conman, scammer or swindler

Feymania: term for conmanship, scam, swindling.

Feymanism: term for conmanship, scam, swindling.

Flop: Pidgin English term for 'full'.

Fon: traditional ruler.

Fondom: people under the jurisdiction of a Fon.

Froc: term used by English-speaking Cameroonians to denigrate their French-speaking compatriots.

Frog: term used by English-speaking Cameroonians to denigrate their French-speaking compatriots.

Fufu: food made out of corn flour.

G

Ga: term for girl; lady

Garri/Gari: Pidgin English language term for flour obtained by grating cassava.

Gata: Pidgin English language term for prison.

Go and go: Pidgin English language expression for 'go away for good'.

Gombo: Pidgin English language term for bribery and corruption

Graffi: an indigene of the Grassfields or bamileke ethnic groups in Cameroon.

Grimba: Pidgin English language term for witchcraft.

Grong beef: a large rat-like animal hunted for food.

H

Haa: Pidgin English language term for strong home-brewed liquor.

Hiish! Pidgin English language interjection that conveys a feeling of repugnance.

Hot: term used when someone wants to drink alcohol rather than a non-alcoholic drink.

Hambok: Pidgin English language term that means worry or trouble someone.

Haricot: Women genitalia.

Helep: Pidgin English term for help.

Hop-eye: Pidgin English term for bullying or coercion

I

Item eleven: Pidgin English expression used to describe food service at a party or social event.

Iki: Local language term expressing surprise.

J

Jama-jama: a generic term for vegetables and greens.
Jambo: Pidgin English expression used in reference to gambling.
Jobajo: Pidgin English word for beer.
Johnny: Pidgin English expression walk.
Jong: Pidgin English expression used to describe someone who is drunk. It also means to drink alcohol.
Juju: Pidgin English word for witch doctor
Jazz: Camfranglais word for beans.
Jim: word culled one of the Bamileke languages. It means big.
Jimtete: a very rich person.
Jongman: Pidgin English expression used to describe a drunk.

K

Kaba: term that refers to a large gown usually worn by women.
Kanas: Pidgin English expression for male genitalia.
Kanda: cowhide prepared for food.
Kati-kati: chicken whose feathers have been removed by passing the bird over a fire.
Kamer: abbreviation for Cameroon/Cameroun.
Kaku: term derived from the English word 'cargo'. It means goods in Cameroon.
Kan-kan: Pidgin English expression for aphrodisiac.
Kick: Pidgin English verb for steal.
Kolo: Camfranglais term that refers to a 1000 francs banknote.
Kongosa: Pidgin English expression for gossip.
Koppo: Pidgin English expression for close friend.
Kosh: Pidgin English expression for insult.
Kwa: Pidgin English expression for handbag.

L

Laf: Pidgin English expression for laugh
Lai: Camfranglais expression for lying or a lie.
Langaa: Pidgin English expression for mouth-watering.
Lass: Pidgin English expression for buttocks and female genitalia.
Lassaman: Pidgin English term of abuse for a stupid person.
Last-born: youngest child in a family.

Let my people go: a fifty percent score on a test or exam/ average performance on a test or exam.

Lewa: Pidgin English expression for school.

Lie-Lie: Pidgin English expression for lies, make-believe and falsehood.

Lolo: large breasts.

Longo-longo: a very tall and skinny person

Long throat: Pidgin English expression for greed.

Lukot: Pidgin English expression for watch out!

M

Magni: mother of twins

Makala-pati: Pidgin English expression for bribery and corruption.

Mami: Pidgin English expression for mother.

Mami–pima: Pidgin English expression that is actually an insult because 'pima' is a Pidgin English word for vagina.

Massa: Pidgin English expression for my friend, man.

Matango: Pidgin English expression for palm-wine.

Match: camfranglais word for sexual intercourse.

Mbambe: hard labor done for a low wage.

Mbutukwu: Pidgin English expression for idiot.

Megan-man: sorcerer; witchdoctor.

Mola: Pidgin English expression for my friend.

Molo-molo: Pidgin English expression for very gently.

N

Nayo: Pidgin English expression for very slowly.

Nchinda: the page of a Fon.

Ndoh: Camfranglais term for money.

Ndomo: Camfranglais term for fight.

Ndutu: Camfranglais term for badluck.

Njanga: Pidgin English term for crayfish.

Nkane: Camfranglais term for prostitute.

Now-Now: Pidgin English expression for immediately.

Nyama-Nyama: Camfranglais term for something of little value/ worthless.

Nyongo: Camfranglais term for witchcraft/ sect/ secret society.

O

Odontol: Pidgin English expression for locally brewed liquor.
Open-eye: Pidgin English expression for bully.
Opep: Pidgin English expression for a car illegally used for transporting passengers.
Over done: Pidgin English expression for someone who overly does something.
Over sabi: one who likes to give the impression that they know more that everyone else.
Owooh! An interjection of surprise or amusement.

P

Pa: term of reverence to the elderly.
Pala-pala: A group fight, especially one involving women.
Palm wine: a type of wine obtained from the palm tree.
Park boy: a self-employed worker who loads and offloads goods at the bus station.
Penia: Duala expression for something brand new.
Penya: Duala expression for something brand new.
Pikin: Pidgin English expression for small child.
Pipo: Pidgin English expression for people.
Poto-poto: Pidgin English expression for mud.
Puff-puff: Pidgin English expression for small friend balls made out of flour.

Q

Quacha: Pidgin English expression for locally brewed alcoholic drink.
Quarter: Pidgin English expression for residential area within a town or village.
Quarter head: elected person who administers a quarter.

R

Raffia-palm wine: drink obtained from the raffia palm.
Red feather: symbol of honor in the village.
Red oil: palm oil
Refre: camfranglais expression for brother
Reme: camfranglais expression for mother.

Repe: camfranglais expression for father.
Rese: camfranglais expression for sister.
Resto: camfranglais expression for restaurant.

S

Saka: Pidgin English expression for dance.
Sancon: flip-flops
Sango: a term of greeting a man.
Sansan boy: a smart boy, a carefree man.
Sapack: A term of abuse.
Sape: The act of dressing well.
Sauveteur: Camfranglais expression for hawker.
Sawa: expression used in reference to tribes of the coastal regions of Cameroon.
Sekele: Camfranglais expression for dance or sexual intercourse.
Sell njangi: expression for an auction of a loan in a traditional loan system.
Shake: to dance
Shap: expression for early in the morning or before the cock crows.
Shiba: Pidgin English expression for criticize, mock or treat someone with scorn.
expression for
Show he! Expression of mockery for someone who doing something wrong.
Sia: Pidgin English expression that means to do something stealthily.
Soya: pidgin word for restaurant grilled meat.
Spare tire: expression for concubine or mistress. See deuxième bureau.
Suffer don finish: Pidgin English expression meaning that there will be no more trouble or hardship.
Swine: Pidgin English expression for pig. It is often used as a term of contempt and as an insult.

T

Taco: Camfranglais word for taxi.

Takumbeng: Pidgin English expression for secret society of Graffi women.

Tara: a way of addressing a friend or person of one's age group.

Tchaka: Camfranglais word for shoes

Tchala: Pidgin English expression for disorder.

Tchapia: To cut down grass on a farm using a cutlass/to violently attack an opponent during a game of soccer.

Tchamassi: a Bamileke traditional music and dance.

Tchinda: a royal page.

Tchoko: Pidgin English expression for bribe.

Tchoronko: Pidgin English expression for a counterfeit telephone.

Tchoukam pass: Pidgin English expression for a loose-living or promiscuous girl or woman.

Throw ngangi: save money in a traditional loan system.

Tobassi: Camfranglais expression for charm.

Toc-toc: Pidgin English expression for a ceremony during which declares his intentions to marry a girl or woman.

Toli: Pidgin English expression for story or gossip.

Ton-ton: Pidgin English expression for the act of being inconsistent; to dilly-dally.

Tory: Pidgin English expression for story or gossip.

Trouble bank: assistance fund/ contingency fund.

Tourne-dos: Camfranglais expression for a roadside restaurant erected on the pavement where people cheap food.

Tum: Camfranglais word that means to sell.

U

Up-eye: Pidgin English expression story or gossip.

V

Vass: Camfranglais word for wash or bathe.

Vex: Pidgin English word for get angry.

Villacon: Camfranglais word for a badly behaved person.

Viveur: Camfranglais word for a fun-loving person/playboy.

Voom: Pidgin English word for bragging or boasting.

Voum: Camfranglais word for bragging or boasting.

W

Waa: Pidgin English word for war.

Wah: Camfranglais word for prostitute; girlfriend.

Walai! Pidgin English expression denoting anger.

Wanda: Camfranglais word for surprise.

Wandaful: Camfranglais expression of astonishment.

Wat: Camfranglais word for caucacian.

Water fufu: term that refers to soaked cassava cooked like fufu.

Way: Camfranglais word for that thing.

Weh-weh! Pidgin English expression denoting surprise.

White mimbo: Pidgin English expression referring to palm or raffia wine.

White stuff: Pidgin English expression referring to palm or raffia wine.

Wolowoss: Camfranglais word for prostitute or loose-living woman.

Womohoh! Interjection denoting pain, surprise, danger and more.

Wowoh: Camfranglais word for bad or unattractive.

Y

Ya: Camfranglais word for hear.

Yaa: Camfranglais interjection for disapproval.

Yam fufu: Pidgin English word for bad or unattractive.

Yemaleh! interjection synonymous with 'gosh'.

Yoh: Camfranglais word for a smart young man.

Yotass: Camfranglais word for money.

Yoyette: Camfranglais word for a smart young woman.

Z

Zangalewa: Camfranglais word for soldier.

Zingué: Camfranglais word for a popular akin to makossa.

Zouazoua: Camfranglais word for gas sold illegally.

Zuazua: Camfranglais word for gas sold illegally.

Chapter 37

Review Activities

In this chapter, readers will avail themselves of practice tasks intended as review activities. Learners are encouraged to resist the temptation of having recourse to the answer key before doing the activities.

EXERCISE 1

The underlined words in the sentences below are wrongly used. Replace them with the appropriate words.

a) This taxi driver is a <u>big</u> fool.
b) Barnabas is a very <u>efficacious</u> teacher.
c) Advil is an <u>efficient</u> drug for the relief of colds and sinusitis.
d) You have to <u>insure</u> that this child is well fed everyday.
e) I wouldn't welcome <u>official</u> interference from anyone.
f) The ex-president will be awarded, an <u>honourable</u> degree in a ceremony at Oxford University.
g) The pupils turned out quite a <u>credible</u> performance.
h) This man has made a fortune in the sale of <u>elicit</u> drugs.
i) This diet is <u>defective</u> in vitamin B.
j) They should adopt a more <u>imaginary</u> approach in solving this problem.

EXERCISE 2

Complete the following sentences by choosing the correct word from the pairs in brackets.

a) My father went on (vacation/vocation) to England.
b) All waste in this house runs into the (sceptic/septic) tank.
c) A (resort/re-sort) is a place where people spend their holidays.
d) I think Sisulu is the most (considerable/considerate) person I've ever met.
e) It is my (destination/destiny) to become president one day.
f) A (glacier/glazier) is someone who fits glass into windows and doors.

g) An (informant/informer) is someone who tells the police that another person has done something unlawful

h) (Antics/antiques) are old objects that are valuable because of their rarity.

i) Finches start to (moult/mould) at around twelve weeks of age.

j) Sexta is an (industrious/industrial) and willing worker.

Chapter 38

Answer Key

Chapter 1
EXERCISE 1

a) Dogs will be brought, treated of fleas and returned to their owners for only one rand.

b) An old lady wants a cleaning job twice a month.

c) Having firmly pierced the oyster with a fork, Peter held it over the fire.

d) The umbrella with brass ribs was misplaced by a teenager.

e) The right thing to do with abusive letters written by children is to throw them into the dustbin.

f) The bottle of wine that was drunk very fast soon got empty.

g) These roughly constructed houses were built about five years ago.

h) If you take your cat on a drive, don't let it hang out of the window when the car in motion.

i) Environmental health crisis: Ad hoc committee to sit and make decisions on how to solve the problem of litter.

j) Sipho and Sons: Dispensing Chemists. We serve you with expertise.

EXERCISE 2

a) Owing to its poor condition, Sifiso was able to buy the car cheap.

b) A female non-smoker is wanted to look after a baby.

c) Mabasa has done hunting and shooting, so he knows what he is talking about.

d) Mash the potato into a pulp if the child would not eat it.

e) The ship disappeared into the water after the Queen Mother had christened it.

f) Mrs. Mbeki expects her fifth child to be back in a couple of months. /Mrs. Mbeki will give birth to her fifth child in a couple of months.

NB: Both answers are acceptable.

g) Using a pistol which he had kept under the pillow, my uncle attempted to kill himself by firing it at his head.

h) Her mother passed away when she was aged two.

i) On her way to fetch water the little girl saw a python.

j) A ghastly accident could be seen as (you/we/they/I) crossed the bridge.

Chapter 2
EXERCISE 1

Now that we have moved into <u>a</u> new millennium, many of us stand at <u>the</u> crossroads. Some of us will have questions on what this new millennium holds in store for us, others about whether they will get jobs or sustain their jobs, whether <u>the</u> sun will shine graciously or will <u>the</u> world plunge into darkness.

Regardless of <u>the</u> time-shift we are experiencing, there is also <u>a</u> call from our Constitution to improve <u>the</u> quality of life of all citizens. Within <u>the</u> Bill of Rights it is clearly written that everyone has inherent dignity and <u>the</u> right to have their dignity respected and protected. Many South Africans have contracted <u>the</u> killer-disease AIDS. It is not for us to be judgemental about such people, but rather our task is to understand what healthy living is about. One could do that by conveying information, beliefs, opinions and feelings. These would show respect for self and others and <u>the</u> ability to advocate personal, family and community health. (Prof. Kader Asmal – *South African Minister of National Education*).

EXERCISE 2

a) The teacher asked the pupils not to make <u>a</u> noise.

b) The speaker made <u>an</u> impression on the audience.

c) The old man didn't make <u>a</u> will before his death.

d) <u>A</u> hundred years ago this town was a village.

e) <u>The</u> Dutch are heavy drinkers.

f) The man makes <u>a</u> fortune by selling drugs.

g) You have made <u>an</u> attempt to improve on your performance.

h) Manamela drank half <u>a</u> glass of wine at the party.

i) <u>The</u> Catholic Church disapproves of abortion.

j) He eats four times <u>a</u> day.

Chapter 3
EXERCISE 1
a) There was a ghastly car accident that led to the <u>death</u> of twenty people.

b) Scientists have proven the <u>non existence</u> of aliens on this planet.

c) We had to pay R200 each to <u>obtain</u> a visa into Swaziland.

d) What your wife did is an <u>inexcusable</u> offence.

e) AIDS is an <u>incurable</u> disease.

f) <u>Often</u>, it is said that <u>ignorance</u> is no excuse in a court of law.

g) Lettie cannot stand her boyfriend's <u>jealousy</u>.

h) The WHO recommends family <u>planning</u> as a birth control strategy.

i) What the minister said at the conference was <u>imprecise</u>.

j) This boy has <u>impregnated</u> his girlfriend.

EXERCISE 2
These days, teenagers are no longer interested in studies. There are so many attractions out there to keep them busy. I find this rather unacceptable because many parents go to all lengths to ensure a better future for their offspring who do not want to do anything else but enjoy themselves. I feel that it is high time these kids listened to parental advice and stop making a fool of themselves. They have to start doing something to better their lives.

EXERCISE 3
a) If we could drive as you do we would have arrived much earlier.

b) In response to this letter, I wish to inform you that the debt has been settled.

c) One feels intimidated when one is closely observed.

d) Her performance was unique this time around.

e) You often commit these errors. You must try to correct them.

f) I believe this is alright for now.

g) I hate this sort of trick.

h) Do you think that is worth doing?

i) Owing to unemployment, our compatriots are emigrating.

j) Your answer is almost correct.

Chapter 4
EXERCISE 1

a) Jenny, would you please pass the salt over to me?

b) The Roman Catholic church frowns on polygamy.

c) John and Helen live in Pretoria.

d) The Muslim feast of Ramadan is celebrated every year.

e) I met a young Belgian in Festival Street on Tuesday. She was looking for Union Buildings.

f) Every June, we visit the Kruger National Park to watch wildlife.

g) My father once lived in Paris, the French capital.

h) I once read a book titled: "To Kill A Man's Pride."

i) It is said that Chaka Zulu was an indomitable warrior.

j) Jesus Christ was the Son of God.

EXERCISE 2
A TALE OF OUR TREE WORLD

My name is Sam. I am ten years old. I like to be out in the veld, to sit on the soft green grass, and to listen to the beetles talking from the bark of trees: the buzz-buzz, sizzing-song that is their way of talking to one another. The woodpecker is here, making woody song right above me: tap, tap, tapping on the bark of a big branch looking for a meal of insects. Sometimes he tap, tap, taps a hole in the branch to make a nest, a nice neat nest, to bring up his family. When I am out of doors in a green place I am so happy! I sit quietly, very quietly, watching the little people of the bush. The ants, they are always busy, going somewhere to find food, or taking care of their own large, very large family. The lizards slide and skate up and down the tree trunk and the rocks. They are a rock and bark colour--you can hardly see them. The spider, the lady spider is spinning her web in which she will catch her meal. The honey worker bees are flying from flower to flower looking for sweet nectar to suck up. (Written by *Sue Hart*)

Chapter 5
EXERCISE 1
a) He is not so stupid to think that some men are superior to others.

b) From Monday you will have to be punctual at work.

c) Paulette says that there was no doubt whether the earth was round.

d) Africa is hard hit by the AIDS pandemic when most people are living in abject poverty.

e) I cannot give you a definite answer at this moment.

f) My younger brother joined the community police force voluntarily.

g) My father lectures at the University of South Africa part-time.

h) Blind people may be taught by means of Braille.

i) People often ignore the importance of environmental care.

j) The price of petrol is higher than it was last year.

EXERCISE 2
a) The consensus is that most people are liars.

b) The policeman said the cause of the accident was drunkenness.

c) The boy wept because his father had died.

d) The shop's closure means that we cannot buy some groceries.

e) I would be late for the meeting as I have had a tyre puncture.

f) My uncle's car is red.

g) Henry's room is rectangular.

h) The crowd at the stadium is small.

i) Outside the parking lot you'll find my bike.

j) This athlete is very tall.

Chapter 6
EXERCISE 1
a) The window of Peter's flat has been broken by thieves.

b) Mary's husband is taller than I am.

c) There is no point in my begging her to marry me.

d) I believe it was he who raped the goat.

e) A family friend of his had an accident with his bike.
f) Blackie and I will not be present at the meeting.
g) Doctor Khumalo plays well.
h) The four pupils started to kick one another.
i) This is the worst march that I have ever seen.
j) My friend wears the same jacket as I wear.

EXERCISE 2
a) Nelson is a man whom everyone can trust.
b) Please tell Susan to give me another novel, I don't like this one.
c) I believe that one should spend one's money judiciously.
d) Who of the two players is better?
e) The three sisters helped one another.
f) Being in haste we/they/he/she/I forgot the car keys.
g) If John would do us this favour, we should be thankful.
h) In our opinion a teacher is never wrong./We think that a teacher is never wrong.
i) School starts at half past eight every day from Monday to Friday.
j) In the end the tourists reached the top of the peak.

Chapter 7
EXERCISE 1
a) Thiza was fined <u>for</u> speeding last weekend.
b) The street kids got used <u>to</u> sleeping in the open air.
c) You do this task <u>at</u> your own risk.
d) Miranda succeeded <u>in</u> convincing him to marry her.
e) I look forward <u>to</u> seeing both of you at the workshop.
f) Salome is bad <u>at</u> mimicking people who stammer.
g) I have great pleasure <u>in</u> informing you that I passed my examination with five distinctions.
h) I read newspapers in order <u>to</u> improve on my communication skills.
i) Nana was praised <u>for</u> her excellent performance at the competition.

j) Are you still keen <u>on</u> joining the newly-formed Democratic Alliance Party?

EXERCISE 2
a) Let me warn you that this is no time <u>for</u> jokes
b) I prefer reading <u>to</u> drinking liquor all the time.
c) She is an authority <u>on</u> gender issues.
d) I am very sensitive <u>to</u> abusive language.
e) There is no means <u>of</u> finding out the truth about the relationship between HIV and AIDS.
f) Msimang had the privilege <u>of</u> being the guest of honour at the function.
g) Your comportment leaves much <u>to</u> be desired.
h) He arrived at the airport <u>in</u> the nick of time.
i) South Africa was disqualified <u>from</u> hosting the 2006 Soccer World Cup.
j) William van Breda is good <u>at</u> cooking the books.

Chapter 8
EXERCISE 1
a) Larry Stengard is the <u>most sinful</u> of the three men.
b) Khosi is the <u>most cruel</u> of the five criminals.
c) Bridget is the <u>most tactless</u> of the four leaders.
d) Euthanasia is the <u>more brutal</u> of the two types of crimes.
e) Irene Aphane is <u>more afraid</u> than her opponent.
f) Arnoldi is <u>more ill</u> today than yesterday.
g) Maryke is the <u>most sly</u> of all the politicians.
h) Moyo's article is the <u>most sordid</u> I ever read.
i) We live in the <u>most appalling</u> conditions.
j) Rebone is the <u>most shy</u> of all my children.

EXERCISE 2
a) Tanya did (worse) than Tselane.
b) Maitland was (more annoyed) than the others.
c) Tsidi is the (most talented) of the three singers.
d) Choh ran (faster) than Bala in the race.
e) Susungi moved (more slowly) than Abe.
f) Lou talks (more loudly) than Echaw.

g) We will know the truth (sooner) rather than (later).
h) He left the hall (more hastily) than expected.
i) Please talk to me in a (less aggressive) manner.
j) Local folks are sometimes (more vocal) than expected.

EXERCISE 3
a) Lilly is the (strongest) girl in the school.
b) James is the (more handsome) of the two brothers.
c) Sue is the (youngest) of all twenty athletes.
d) Jill is the (oldest) of all the ten boxers.
e) Yours is the (best) story so far.
f) Which of the two do you like (more), tea or coffee?
g) Gold is the (most expensive) of the precious stones.
h) The Zambezi is the (longest) river in this part of Africa.
i) Georgette is (worse) than her sister.
j) Which of the six trees is the (tallest)?

Chapter 9
EXERCISE 1
a) Is bread and cheese on the table?
b) Was the bread and jam eaten?
c) The news was shocking.
d) The council (has or have) published the annual report.
NB: Both are acceptable because a collective noun is singular when the group acts a group. It is plural when it refers to individual members of the group.
e) The board (is or are) sitting today. NB: Same as (d).
f) Mpho's pants (are) torn in the right leg.
g) She went to fetch a pair of pliers that (was) in the cupboard.
h) One of the women (was) guilty.
i) A range of goods (was) bought from Sunnypark.
j) All along the road (lie) traces of blood.

EXERCISE 2
a) Joseph is one of those who (think) so much about riches.
b) Mathematics (is) my favourite subject at school.
c) Jonas or Sedibana (is) leaving for overseas tomorrow.

d) Either he or she (is) wrong.
e) Not only I but also they (are) right.
f) Liza as well as her brothers (was) invited for dinner.
g) Many a tourist (has) been killed in this country.
h) Three-quarters of the farm (is) arid.
i) Nothing but protea (grows) here.
j) Their aim and objective (is) to make progress.

EXERCISE 3
a) Sports (are) necessary for a healthy body.
b) This series of articles (is) quite informative.
c) Three hours' play (was) enough for me.
d) There (has) been one or two volcanic eruptions this year.
e) A minimum of fifty credits (is) required to be admitted to sit the examination.
f) Two-thirds of the animals (were) killed by the tornado.
g) The corps of soldiers (was) victorious.
h) The greater part of those three weeks of vacation (was) spent at the Kruger National Park.
i) The committee (has or have) arrived at a consensus. NB: Same as (d) and (e) in exercise 1.
j) A mob of vagrants (has) taken the city by storm.

Chapter 10
EXERCISE 1
a) Barry will have to bring <u>some more</u> money in order to complete his payment for the car.
b) Brownwell invited all his friends to a birthday party but <u>few</u> came.
c) Do you like milk in your coffee, Brendan? Yes, just <u>a little</u>.
d) Donald Cook gave Hubert a strong cup of coffee, saying that there was <u>little</u> milk left.
e) Wallmach complained that <u>all</u> the clothes had been stolen.
f) All the streets in Hammanskraal have potholes.
g) <u>The whole (entire)</u> street was flooded after the downpour.
h) Kim stressed that a caring mother wouldn't hit <u>any</u> of her children.

i) Whenever Johan enters <u>a</u> shop, he buys something.

j) Coetzee has eaten the <u>whole</u> cake.

EXERCISE 2

a) Tepla thinks that there is no restaurant in Messina.

b) "That's all; I have no other point to make," said the minister.

c) Katz told me that there were four actresses taking part in the play.

d) Horton feels that we must find two other colours to match these two.

e) Brandon said that fifty more pupils were admitted into their school at the end of last term.

f) McCarron says you are making too much noise in this room.

g) It gives me much pleasure to be given this opportunity to address you this evening.

h) Dubois spends much of her time signing documents.

i) Matthew Weir pointed out that there is plenty of rich land in his village.

J) Gunter was detained, the rest of the offenders were set free.

EXERCISE 3

a) Mary hasn't much food left.

b) Are there many clothes in the wardrobe?

c) There isn't much money available, my boy.

d) Does Benny take much interest in sport?

e) Manu hasn't much time left.

f) Dudu tell me, are there so many students in class?

g) How many people are absent today?

h) There hasn't been much sunshine these days.

i) He doesn't know much French.

j) Many drops of water can fill a bucket.

Chapter 11
EXERCISE 1

a) Maria does not like <u>your</u> leaving late at night.

b) You should sneak out without <u>his</u> noticing.

c) Taking part in a competition is more important than <u>winning</u>.

d) <u>Losing</u> is no disgrace.

e) I expect that not <u>knowing</u> the answer does not surprise you.
f) <u>Washing</u> and <u>ironing</u> clothes takes a lot of time.
g) <u>Reading</u> helps me to relax.
h) <u>Sunbathing</u> can be very dangerous at times.
i) I hope <u>my</u> arriving late does not inconvenience you.
j) Molema enjoys <u>reading</u> adventure stories.
k) I hate <u>his</u> working so late at night.
l) Prof. Kruger dislikes <u>your</u> talking so loudly in the corridors.

EXERCISE 2
a) beginning
b) writing
c) lying
d) canoeing
e) manoeuvring
f) competing
g) fulfilling
h) believing
i) receiving
j) escaping

EXERCISE 3
a) We were told of your <u>coming</u>.
b) Do you mind my <u>taking</u> off these shoes?
c) Beverley goes there at the risk of <u>being</u> killed.
d) Miyeni risks <u>losing</u> her job.
e) The taxi will be long in <u>coming</u>.
f) Mogale enjoys <u>staring</u> at passersby.
g) Mbewe has the duty of <u>setting</u> a good example.
h) Since the rebuke, Maja has abstained from <u>smoking</u>.
i) <u>Gazing</u> at the examination timetable will do you no good.
j) This youngster likes <u>kissing</u> his puppy.

Chapter 12
EXERCISE 1

NB: Teachers must use their discretion here. However, the grammatical correctness of each sentence is an imperative.

EXERCISE 2
a) beau/bough
b) paws/pores
c) course/coarse
d) grate/great
e) wry/rye
f) use/ewes
g) cession/session
h) sole/soul
i) seize/cease
j) quay/key

Chapter 13
EXERCISE 1
a) Things are not always as attractive as they appear.
b) He is jealous.
c) To argue about insignificant things.
d) To spend all one's earnings; to make no provision for the future.
e) Strict rules.
f) To act treacherously; to play both sides.
g) To be afraid.
h) By fair means or foul.
i) At the last moment.
j) In an extremely short time.
k) Think carefully before acting.
l) Everything summed up in a few words.
m) Not measuring up to required standard.
n) To express in very concise terms.
o) To make peace.
p) To ask for peace.
q) To pay the expenses.
r) To analyse critically.
s) To rely on.
t) To happen.

EXERCISE 2
a) Judas a won a prize but I drew a blank.
b) A shrewd businessman will bid his time before he acts.
c) I am sorry if that remark hurt you, but if the cap fits wear it.
d) When it comes to risks no one is prepared to bell the cat.
e) What are you going to get out of her if you continue to rub up the wrong way?

Chapter 14
EXERCISE 1
a) <u>To swim</u> is pleasant in summer.
b) They decided <u>to return</u> to school.
c) My ambition is <u>to become</u> a teacher.
d) He was about <u>to speak</u> when I interrupted him.
e) Robert was determined <u>to master</u> the art of windsurfing.
f) "<u>To be</u> or not <u>to be</u>" that is the question.
g) I wanted <u>to escape</u> from here but he stopped me.
h) We asked Don <u>to go</u> to the cinema.
i) You have <u>to listen</u> to your parents.
j) He had the urge <u>to blow</u> up the aircraft.

EXERCISE 2
a) Don't let Jimmy go all by himself.
b) She made me write the sentence thrice in my workbook.
c) I couldn't help laughing when she told me the story.
d) Johnny made her feel unwanted.
e) I heard him open the door at midnight.

Chapter 15
EXERCISE 1
a) A book in which the events of each day are recorded is a <u>diary</u>.
b) A book containing information on all branches of knowledge is an <u>encyclopaedia</u>.
c) An extract or selection from a book an <u>excerpt</u>.
d) Language which is confusing and unintelligible is <u>jargon</u>.
e) A declaration of the plans and promises put forward by a candidate for election, political party or sovereign is a <u>manifesto</u>.

f) An error in printing or misprint is an <u>erratum</u>.

g) The exclusive right of an author or his/her heirs to publish or sell copies of his/her writings is <u>copyright</u>.

h) Passing off another author's work as one's own is <u>plagiarism</u>.

i) A record of one's life written by oneself is an <u>autobiography</u>.

j) The history of the life of a person is a <u>biography</u>.

EXERCISE 2

a) The study of birds is called <u>ornithology</u>.

b) The study of stars is called <u>astronomy</u>.

c) The natural history of animals is called <u>zoology</u>.

d) The study of ancient buildings and prehistoric remains is called <u>archaeology</u>.

e) The art of cultivating and managing gardens is called <u>horticulture</u>.

f) The study of rocks and soils is called <u>geology</u>.

g) The study of humankind is called <u>anthropology</u>.

h) The science of colours is called <u>chromatics</u>.

i) The scientific study of industrial arts is called <u>technology</u>.

j) The science of the structure of the human body is called <u>anatomy</u>.

Chapter 16
EXERCISE 1

a) The dog leapt out of its <u>kennel</u> and bit the passerby.

b) A <u>playwright</u> is a writer of plays.

c) An <u>epigram</u> is a short sarcastic saying or poem.

d) <u>Procrastination</u> is the thief of time.

e) Eve was tempted by a <u>serpent</u> in the garden of Eden.

f) All the students are <u>satisfied</u> with their marks.

g) An <u>octogenarian</u> is a person who is between eighty and eighty-nine years old.

h) A <u>cypher</u> is a secret system of writing that you can use to send messages (also spelt <u>cipher</u>).

i) <u>Quadruplets</u> are four children born to the same mother at the same time.

j) <u>Confetti</u> is thrown on people at weddings.

EXERCISE 2
a) The dinosaur is a large reptile that is <u>extinct</u> now.
b) The act of marrying many wives is called <u>polygamy</u>.
c) <u>Underwear</u> means the clothes that we wear under our clothes.
d) Some people were put to death by <u>electrocution</u>.
e) An admiral is a senior officer who commands a navy <u>or fleet</u> of ships.
f) The doctor felt the patients <u>pulse</u>.
g) A <u>corpse</u> is a dead person.
h) I cannot read your handwriting; it is <u>illegible</u>.
i) Doctors generally use <u>clinical</u> thermometers.
j) Louis XIV of France was <u>guillotined</u>.

Chapter 17
EXERCISE 1
a) <u>Leaning</u> forward and <u>kicking</u> the horse, the rider raced at top speed.
b) Thirsty and <u>exhausted</u>, the travellers who had <u>lost</u> their way in the forest <u>moved</u> on.
c) The parrot kept on <u>screeching</u> and <u>craning</u> its neck.
d) We had hardly <u>taken</u> a step when the hyena started to howl.
e) I could have sworn I had <u>seen</u> nothing.
f) There was nothing to break the silence of the night except the beating of our hearts.
g) Even the police-dog has little chance of finding the wounded animal.
h) The lady was all excited and shaking like a leaf.
i) By the time the flames died out I had fallen asleep.
j) The animal must have sensed danger.

EXERCISE 2
a) <u>Marrying</u> two wives is unacceptable in some churches.
b) Lingering is another word for <u>hanging</u> about.
c) In some buses <u>smoking</u> is not allowed.
d) <u>Pampering</u> is a synonym for petting.
e) An <u>itching</u> is a ticklish feeling.

f) <u>Ruminating</u> animals bring back food from their stomach into their mouth and chew it again.

g) Baba was away when the crime was <u>committed</u>.

h) A dog leapt out of its kennel and <u>barked</u> furiously at the stranger.

i) Genetically <u>modified</u> food is not good for our health.

j) All the teachers are <u>satisfied</u> with the pupils' performance.

Chapter 18
EXERCISE 1

a) <u>Civil</u> servants will <u>receive</u> the news with great joy.

b) The male will be <u>replaced</u> by the female.

c) What you have done is not <u>clear</u> at all.

d) A computer <u>can</u> do <u>multiplication.</u>

e) I took a <u>nice photograph</u> of that building yesterday.

f) The <u>public</u> is hereby informed that the library will be closed from 14h00-16h00 tomorrow.

g) I want to built a house for myself next year.

h) Your English language <u>accent</u> is not <u>accurate</u>.

i) This <u>horrible</u> behaviour is very <u>disgraceful</u>.

j) This is quite a <u>complicated</u> problem.

EXERCISE 2

a) This is the dawn of the new <u>millennium</u>.

b) Nhlapo has all ready booked for his accommodation.

c) We are trying to <u>integrate environmental</u> education into the new curriculum.

d) Cliff Olivier has stressed the <u>importance</u> of <u>environmental health</u>.

e) Derick du Toit can do a lot of things, for <u>instance</u>, drive cook and dance.

f) <u>We are</u> totally committed to this cause.

g) Muller stands to <u>benefit</u> from this project.

h) Pat Venter didn't have a <u>bath</u> for the <u>whole</u> week.

i) Phuti has made an error of <u>omission</u>.

j) Ladies and gentlemen, you are all very <u>welcome</u> to this occasion.

EXERCISE 3

Every <u>second</u> of every day <u>babies</u> are born all over the world. This means that <u>more</u> people are <u>depending</u> on the earth and its <u>natural</u> <u>resources</u> to <u>provide</u> them with what they need to <u>survive</u>. It is <u>therefore important</u> for us all and <u>future</u> generations to learn to <u>appreciate</u> these <u>resources</u>. We are a throw-away <u>nation</u>, our planet is becoming a huge <u>dump</u>.

Chapter 19
EXERCISE 1

a) A group of well-dressed youngsters were strolling in the street.

b) In view of the circumstances, Mr. Smit has kept remarkably cheerful.

c) Bentley was arrested after a police raid.

d) On the battlefield the tanks that had exploded prevented the advance of troops.

e) Although it is sometimes unreliable, Sebueng depends on the bus service.

f) Some countries, such as Kenya, have exceptionally high mountains.

g) Preparation for the conference required hard work not only by men but also by women.

h) The election resulted not only in the death of apartheid but also in the birth of democracy in South Africa.

i) Delport said he would call either the next day or the day after.

j) Etienne has neither phoned nor written.

EXERCISE 2

a) Willis can speak German very well.

b) Carla likes exotic music very much.

c) As a beginner, Jan cannot speak French perfectly.

d) Deon explained the maths problem very clearly.

e) Richard shot a lion with a gun last week.

f) Caiphus put the money into his pocket.

g) Notshaya dislikes red wine very much.

h) Mgidlana learned the poems by heart.

i) Vald received a Christmas gift from his uncle.

j) Norman quickly shut the door of his shack.

Chapter 20
EXERCISE 1

a) Molema <u>did not</u> go home yesterday.

b) Papo <u>did not</u> tell us to wait there.

c) Maishamaite <u>did not</u> make a mistake during the mid-year exam.

d) Pieter <u>did not</u> break the window deliberately.

e) Betty <u>did not</u> do the assignment in a desultory manner.

f) Babe <u>does not</u> speak Zulu very fluently.

g) Emmerencia <u>did not</u> buy a new hat at Spar.

h) Mark <u>did not</u> find his missing book.

i) Terence <u>did not</u> arrive late from home.

j) Kennedy <u>does not</u> know the answer.

EXERCISE 2

a) No, my father did not buy a BMW.

b) No, my younger brother does not know how to swim.

c) No, she didn't find her shoes.

d) No, it was not the prefect who rang the bell.

e) No, the professor did not teach anything new.

f) No, the president did not fly to New York last week.

g) No, they did not solve the problem for me.

h) No, my mother does not speak many languages.

i) No, it doesn't look like rain.

j) No, the cops did not arrest the thief.

EXERCISE 3

a) Lynne could find Harry nowhere/Lynne could not find Harry anywhere.

b) There isn't anyone who knows the whereabouts of Epie.

c) Bill didn't see anybody in the hall/Bill saw nobody in the hall.

d) Mbongeni did not tell me anything/Mbongeni told me nothing.

e) Mondlane is neither wise nor foolish.

f) Stephen will find the money nowhere/Stephen will not find the money anywhere.

g) We did not give Trodger anything/We gave Trodger nothing.

h) Thebe doesn't know anything in mathematics/Thebe knows nothing in mathematics.

i) Charmaine did not speak to anyone in the crowd/Charmaine spoke to no-one in the crowd.

j) Nobody ever saw him with Belinda.

Chapter 21
EXERCISE 1
a) hoofs
b) turfs
c) wharfs
d) knives
e) cupfuls
f) passersby
g) secretaries
h) crises
i) theses
j) analyses
k) oases
l) banjos
m) commandos
n) gechos
o) atlases
p) larvae
q) alibis
r) mottoes
s) cargoes
t) dominoes

EXERCISE 2
a) beaux
b) plateaux
c) bureaux
d) mesdames
e) messieurs
f) focuses/foci
g) funguses/fungi
h) stimuluses/stimuli
i) stadiums/stadia
j) phenomena
k) lice
l) mice
m) matrices
n) vortices
o) indexes/indices
p) criteria
q) automata
r) data
s) memoranda
t) errata

Chapter 22
EXERCISE 1
a) Bra Gibba was born <u>in</u> 1994.

b) <u>In</u> summer the weather is very hot in this part of the world.
c) <u>On</u> Christmas Day, Sandile received many gifts from friends.
d) Khoza and his wife arrived <u>at</u> the Johannesburg International Airport at 3p.m.
e) There is a conference in Nairobi <u>on</u> October 15, 2000.
f) Msibi often returns home <u>at</u> noon for lunch.
g) <u>In</u> winter the weather is terribly cold in South Africa.
h) The car will be brought back <u>on</u> Tuesday.
i) <u>In</u> the afternoon I will go and fetch the mail.
j) I bought this suit <u>for</u> five thousand rands.

EXERCISE 2
a) Thiza, someone is knocking <u>on</u> the door.
b) Tsepo is searching for his lost book.
c) Ngwane explained the problem to me very well.
d) Nakedi never listens <u>to</u> her father.
e) Cosmas responded <u>to</u> my question immediately.
f) Shandu is in a hurry, he cannot <u>for</u> wait us.
g) Mbeki asked <u>for</u> my calculator yesterday but hasn't returned it.
h) Njabulo pointed <u>at</u> the lunatic and broke into a run.
i) Sithole was charged <u>with</u> rape.
j) Pearl was accused <u>of</u> stealing by her friends.

Chapter 23
EXERCISE 1
a) Anne-Marie said I was <u>foolish</u> to accept such an offer.
b) Cohen is such a <u>miserly</u> person.
c) Mr. Payne spent the entire afternoon <u>alone</u>.
d) Mr. Kirkegaard behaves <u>in a friendly manner</u>.
e) Mrs. Kamper is such a <u>truthful</u> woman.
f) Lenjo's car is worth R100 million.
g) The lame man <u>is not able</u> to climb the stairs.
h) Lebeloane has <u>weighed</u> the luggage.
i) Roger Miller plays soccer very <u>well</u>.
j) Awoonor sang quite <u>beautifully</u> this morning in church.

EXERCISE 2
a) <u>Are</u> you not afraid of the lions?
b) The little boy has <u>lost</u> his ball.
c) The pupil has <u>passed</u> his examination very well.
d) The athlete ran <u>past</u> us.
e) He gave me a good piece of <u>advice</u>.
f) You <u>were</u> first to greet the professor.
g) The number of newspapers published in this country <u>is</u> increasing.
NB: (This sentence was correct initially).
h) The <u>poor</u> say that money cannot buy happiness.
i) I <u>have been</u> waiting for two hours now.
j) I have <u>much work</u> to do this night before going to bed.

Chapter 24
EXERCISE 1
a) He invited us <u>to discuss</u> the match fixtures.
b) I was lucky <u>since</u> my friend was living in France and spoke French fluently.
c) The department is reviewing its policy <u>on</u> immunisation.
d) This is a question that has been asked several times <u>concerning</u> (about) our foreign policy.
e) I am calling <u>to talk about</u> your article on media racism.
f) The suit cost me <u>about</u> R1000-00.
g) <u>In its context</u>, your statement has a deep meaning.
h) <u>The inadequate supply</u> of meat is resented in some quarters.
i) You need to resolve this problem <u>urgently</u> (as soon as possible).
j) Most parents are generally helpless <u>concerning</u> (as regards) the sexual behaviour of their children.
EXERCISE 2
a) To go <u>on</u> a sight-seeing trip.
b) To make the best of the time <u>at</u> one's disposal. NB: (This sentence was correct initially).
c) To travel <u>at</u> one's own risk.
d) To go <u>on</u> a conducted tour.

NB: (This sentence was correct initially).
e) To have a look <u>at</u> a hotel guide.
NB: (This sentence was correct initially).
f) To book accommodation <u>in</u> advance.
g) To be tired <u>of</u> waiting.
h) To undertake an extensive tour <u>of</u> the country.
i) To admire works <u>of</u> art at leisure.
j) To obtain a temporary visa <u>to</u> enter a country.

Chapter 25
EXERCISE 1
a) Let <u>he</u> and <u>she</u> go to the movie.
b) Jeanne wished <u>us</u> a safe journey.
c) Roselyn made <u>them</u> repeat the sentence thrice.
d) All the panellists greed except <u>him</u>.
e) I knew the girl to be <u>she</u>.
f) Those like <u>him</u> are always getting in trouble.
g) Javas did better than <u>I</u> this time.
h) Hazel likes you more than <u>me</u>.
i) Basil and Nomsa ran faster than <u>us</u>.
j) Mthembu gave you less than <u>she</u>.

EXERCISE 2
a) Mashoeng is the man <u>who</u> they thought was a thief.
b) Is she the girl <u>who</u> you think is a spy?
c) Nkosi is the lady <u>who</u> they believe I am going to marry.
d) That is the wife of the man <u>who</u> (that) was injured.
e) The child next to <u>whom</u> you are sitting is very ill.
f) Is it Mary-Jane's car <u>that</u> was stolen?
g) This is the problem that (which) we have to solve urgently.
h) <u>All animals</u> that graze on fynbos are usually healthy.
i) Titanic was the best film <u>that</u> I had ever watched.
j) This is the best thriller <u>that</u> I have read in my life.

Chapter 26
EXERCISE 1

"Hear how kind Mr. Bons is," said his mother. While his father said:

"Very well, let him say his poem, and that will do. He is going to my sister on Tuesday and she will cure him of his alley- slopering (laughter). Say your poem."

The boy began. "Standing aloof in giant ignorance." His father laughed again— roared.

"One for you, my son! Standing aloof in giant ignorance! I never knew these poets talked sense. Just describes you."

"Here, Bons, you go in for poetry. Put him through it will you, while I fetch the whisky."

"Yes, give me the Keats," said Mr. Bons. "Let him say his Keats to me."

So for a very short moment the wise man and the ignorant boy were left alone in the smoking room.

"Standing aloof in ignorance of these I dream of the Cyclades as one who sits ashore and longs perchance to visit-

"Quite right. To visit what?"

"To visit the dolphin coral deep seas," said the boy, and burst into tears.

"Come, come! Why do you cry?"

"Because—because all these words that only rhymed before, now that I've come back they're me."

Mr. Bons laid the Keats down.

The case was more interesting than he had expected.

"You? he exclaimed. This sonnet you?"

"Yes—and look further on: Aye, on the shores of darkness there is light, and precipices show untrodden green. It is so, sir. All these things are true."

"I never doubted it, said Mr. Bons, with closed eyes.

"You—then you believe me? You believe in the omnibus and the driver and the storm, that return ticket I got for nothing and—"

"Tut, tut! No more of your yarns my boy. I meant that I never doubted the essential truth of poetry. Some day when you have read more you will understand what I mean."

"But Mr. Bons it is so. There is light upon the shores of darkness. I have seen it coming. Light and a wind."

"Nonsense," said Mr. Bons. (*E. M. Forster*)

EXERCISE 2
a) Kere was so tired that he could not walk.
b) Why did Bongani go to bed so early?
c) "You can go wherever you want," said my mother.
d) I wonder where Fabian could be now.
e) I don't know the house in which Simphiwe was born.
f) What the hell is going on here!
g) These are the shoes that Sonnyboy wore on Sunday.
h) Mike went to Spar and bought some foodstuff: rice, mealie, potatoes and meat.
i) Which train goes to Grahamstown?
j) Each player will receive a cash prize of R30,000.

Chapter 27
EXERCISE 1
a) Enoch is <u>very</u> angry because you did not come to his party yesterday.
b) Sontonga was <u>very</u> pleased to meet the president.
c) Yvonne was <u>much</u> afraid of being raped.
d) That was a <u>very</u> amusing tale.
e) Thembi looks <u>very</u> tired today.
f) Ernest plays <u>much</u> better than his opponents.
g) Bongi's essay is <u>much</u> worse than mine.
h) Brian was <u>very</u> interested to hear the outcome of the match.
i) Nomonde was <u>very</u> astonished at the news.
j) That was a <u>very</u> meaningful poem.

EXERCISE 2
a) Mohammed likes grapes <u>very much.</u>
b) We cannot study in this room, there is <u>too much</u> noise.
c) Fifty rands is <u>too much</u> for this book.
d) Cindy drank <u>too much</u> at party and felt sick the following day.
e) Chester talks <u>too much</u>: he is a chatterbox.
f) We were <u>very much</u> amazed to hear that he died suddenly.

g) Ndoumbe is <u>very much</u> obliged to you.
h) Thank you <u>very much</u> for the service you've rendered us.
i) Gugu was <u>very much</u> interested in AIDS education.
j) Ngema has helped me <u>very much</u>.

Chapter 28
EXERCISE 1

He wanted to know if she liked Tom. She replied that she did.
He asked if Rex lived there. She replied that he did not.
He asked if she had met Keith. She replied that she had not.
He asked if she would marry him. She replied that she would.
(Cathy Pienaar, 1994)

EXERCISE 2

The president said that he was very glad to tell them that the asbestos company had made a remarkable success in the course of the previous year. He further pointed out that sales and production had risen dramatically from a record low the year before and that their plants had undergone thorough overhaul. He hoped that in the coming year they would buy new machines in order to boost their productivity and trusted that customers would appreciate that.

EXERCISE 3

a) "Would you like a cup of tea, Paulette?" Paul asked.
b) "Do you like going to the movie?" he inquired.
c) "We wonder if the pupils have written a test."
d) "Shut the door, will you?" my father said.
e) "Don't stare at me," said Hilda.
f) "You have to stop worrying," Napoleon said.
g) "Where are my keys?" asked Pastor Cosmas.
h) "What's the time?" Janet asked.
i) "I wish I knew where Rina lives," Albertina said.
j) "I wish I knew what you are busy at," Tomboya said.

Chapter 29
EXERCISE 1

a) Noah is one of the men who <u>were</u> chosen.
b) Here is one of the cars that <u>were</u> stolen.
c) This green box is one of the boxes that are empty.

d) Vincent is the chap who broke into my house.
e) Barry and <u>I</u> went to the beach last weekend.
f) <u>They</u> and I will visit the game reserve next month.
g) It's <u>we</u> who ran the marathon a couple of months ago.
h) It's <u>I</u> who drank your coffee.
i) It is not <u>they</u> who killed the thief.
j) It was <u>she</u> who won the beauty contest.

EXERCISE 2
a) The car belongs to my brother and <u>me</u>.
b) <u>You</u> and <u>I</u> can tow the car away.
c) To <u>whom</u> does this book belong?
d) She is a writer <u>whom</u> many people enjoy reading.
e) The man to <u>whom</u> you have to complain is Marcela.
f) Fourie is the candidate <u>whom</u> you ought to vote for.
g) Stacey is the one <u>who</u> I think saw what happened.
h) They nominated someone <u>who</u> they believe was responsible enough to do the job.
i) There is some uncertainty about <u>who</u> should be chosen.
j) <u>Who</u> else did you meet at the party?

Chapter 30
EXERCISE
a) If I <u>were</u> you I would decline the offer.
b) If my father <u>were</u> here he would know what to do in the present circumstances.
c) If he <u>were</u> king he would marry many wives.
d) I wish my mother <u>were</u> here now to alleviate my suffering.
e) That <u>will</u> depend on whether she is convinced or not.
f) It <u>would</u> be pointless to try to persuade them.

Chapter 31
EXERCISE 1
a) blindness   k) clock
b) boxer   l) complaining
c) brief   m) full
d) avoid   n) greedy

e) beggar
f) blameless
g) congratulation
h) compel
i) countless
j) conquer

o) huge
p) lazy
q) hatred
r) huge
s) friendship
t) fake/false

EXERCISE 2
a) As angry as a wasp.
b) As blind as a bat.
c) As blue as indigo.
d) As big as an elephant
e) As ancient as sun/the stars.
f) As brave as Achilles.
g) As cheerless as a grave.
h) As clear as daylight/crystal/a bell/rock water.
i) As docile as a lamb.
j) As deceitful as a devil.
k) As dark as a dungeon.
l) As cunning as a fox/monkey.
m) As countless as stars/hair/desert sands.
n) As complacent as a cat.
o) As contrary as light and dark.
p) As devoted as a faithful dog.
q) As eager as a bridegroom.
r) As friendly as a puppy.
s) As glad as a fly/blooming tree.
t) As gloomy as night.

Chapter 32
EXERCISE 1
a) We advocate placing girls on equality with boys.
b) The company's activities are not limited to paper production.
c) Hard work and hard work alone is the thing that counts.
d) Muma is as clever as Janet.
e) Terre Blanche fell off his horse.

f) He lied because he was scared/The reason for his lying is that he was scared.

g) We met in Kempton Park long ago.

h) You are nearer Joseph's age than your sister is.

i) It is imperative that we cooperate to fight the AIDS pandemic. / It is imperative that we work together to fight the AIDS pandemic.

j) The minister has returned to Pretoria after attending the conference in Durban. / The minister has gone back to Pretoria after attending the conference in Durban.

EXERCISE 2

a) Our progress was delayed when Dreyer reversed the car.

b) Let's together give thanks that this bachelor is now being married to this lovely girl.

c) This hall is filled to capacity because the film on is known internationally. / The hall is filled to capacity because the film on is known all over the world.

d) Advertisement: Just circle the block on our new skateboard once and we are sure you will want to repeat the experience.

e) Advertisement: Our new product kills flies and ants and yet it contains no poison.

f) Advertisement: All our prices have been reduced today so come in and receive a gift at the door.

g) For those people who are out of work, the government is offering help.

h) Right now, a boring TV show is being advertised as a wonderful innovation in the art of the mini-series. / At the moment, a boring TV show is being advertised as a wonderful innovation in the art of the mini-series.

Chapter 33
EXERCISE 1

a) Here is a box <u>containing</u> several tools.

b) People <u>living</u> in remote areas seldom come to the city.

c) Daniel bought some provisions <u>including</u> soap, omo, dish-washing liquid, foam-bath and toilet tissue.

d) There is a five-meter fence <u>enclosing</u> the school.

e) AIDS is a viral disease <u>affecting</u> intravenous drug users.

f) A barrage is a large wall across a river <u>making</u> a sort of dam for irrigation.

g) Soil is the thin layer of the ground <u>consisting</u> of tiny particles of rock, rotted plants and some living organisms.

h) Plasma is the clear fluid part of blood <u>comprising</u> the corpuscles and cells.

i) A pentagon is a figure <u>having</u> five sides.

j) We saw a man <u>wearing</u> a leopard skin waistcoat.

EXERCISE 2

a) Ten o'clock <u>was</u> my father's busiest time.

b) The orphans <u>had</u> to be bathed and fed.

c) The police-men <u>were</u> going to the gangster's house.

d) The rapist <u>had been</u> hiding behind the wall at night.

e) A new shop <u>had been</u> opened around the corner.

f) You <u>could</u> buy provisions cheap at <u>that</u> supermarket.

g) Many pedestrians <u>had been</u> killed by drunk drivers.

h) We <u>planned</u> to visit the Zambezi at our earliest convenience.

i) My sister <u>liked</u> winter so much.

j) You <u>needed</u> a visa in order to visit Botswana.

EXERCISE 3

a) The accused has <u>committed</u> several crimes.

b) They were <u>sentenced</u> to imprisonment.

c) I <u>pleaded</u> not guilty.

d) My aunt was <u>defended</u> by a lawyer.

e) Counsel for the defense <u>contradicted</u> many witnesses.

f) They <u>testified</u> under oath that the accused was innocent.

g) One of the offenders <u>contradicted</u> himself when crossed-questioned.

h) The prosecutor insisted that the accused was guilty and <u>asked</u> for a conviction.

i) The magistrate <u>let</u> the accused off with a warning.

j) The attorney said that it could not be <u>proved</u> beyond reasonable doubt that the accused was guilty.

Chapter 34
EXERCISE 1
told said saying think insists ask believes demanding like notified

EXERCISE 2
a) will
b) will
c) will
d) will
e) shall
f) will
g) will
h) will
i) shall
j) shall

Chapter 35
EXERCISE 1
a) This taxi driver is a <u>great</u> fool.
b) Barnabas is a very <u>efficient</u> teacher.
c) Advil is an <u>effective</u> drug for the relief of colds and sinusitis.
d) You have to <u>ensure</u> that this child is well fed everyday.
e) I wouldn't welcome <u>officious</u> interference from anyone.
f) The ex-president will be awarded an <u>honorary</u> degree in a ceremony at Oxford University.
g) The pupils turned out quite a <u>creditable</u> performance.
h) This man has made a fortune in the sale of <u>illicit</u> drugs.
i) This diet is <u>deficient</u> in vitamin B.
j) They should adopt a more <u>imaginative</u> approach in solving this problem.

EXERCISE 2
a) My father went on <u>vacation</u> to England.
b) All waste in this house runs into the <u>septic</u> tank.
c) A <u>resort</u> is a place where people spend their holidays.
d) I think Sisulu is the most <u>considerate</u> person I've ever met.
e) It is my <u>destiny</u> to become president one day.

f) A glazier is someone who fits glass into windows and doors.

g) An informer is someone who tells the police that another person has done something unlawful.

h) Antiques are old objects that are valuable because of their rarity.

i) Finches start to moult at around twelve weeks of age.

j) Sexta is an industrious and willing worker.

Selected Bibliography

Ayafor, M. and Green, M. (2017). *Cameroon Pidgin English: A Comprehensive Grammar.* Amsterdam: John Benjamins Publishing Company.

Best, D. Wilfred. (1983). *The Students' Companion.* London: Collins.

Bobda, S.A and Mbangwana, P. (1993). *An Introduction to Spoken English.* Lagos: University of Lagos Press.

Boulton, Margorie. (1960). *The Anatomy of Language: Saying what we mean.* London: Routledge & Kegan Paul.

Brooks, B.A.et al. (1988). *Insights: English First Language.* Kenwyn: Juta & Co. Ltd.

Butias, J. (1990). *A Guide to the use of English.* Lagos: Maalsum Publishing Company.

Cleary, Sandra et al. (1992). *The Communication Handbook.* Kenwyn: Juta & Co. Ltd.

Collins Cobuild. (1989). *Dictionary of Phrasal Verbs.* London: William Collins Sons & Ltd.

_____ (1992). *English Usage.* London: Harper Collins Publishers Ltd.

Cretchley.Gail and Stacey, Jennifer. (1994). *Write Well: Skills for Better English.* Randburg: Ravan Press (Pty) Ltd.

Davis, Edwardo. (1972). *Introduction to Modern English Usage.* CapeTown: Oxford University Press.

Etherton, A. R. B. (1978). *Mastering Modern English: A Certificate Course.* London: Longman.

Fitikides, T. J. (1984). *Common Mistakes in English.* London: Longman.

Fletcher, E. & Swanepoel, W. J. (1969). *New English as a Second Language(Book One).*Cape Town: Maskew Miller Ltd.

Fonkoua, H.K. *(2015) A Dictionary of Camfranglais.* Frankfurt am Main: Peter Lang.

Fowler, H. W. (1965). *A Dictionary of Modern English Usage.* Oxford: Oxford University Press.

Freeman, William. (1967*). A Concise Dictionary of English Idioms.* London: The English Universities Press Ltd.

Gower, Ernest. (1979). *The Complete Plain Words.* Middlesex: Penguin Books.

Heaton, J.B. (1984). *Prepositions and Adverbial Particles.* Essex: Longman.

Hopwood, D. and Standard, M. (1974). *English the Active Way.* Kenwyn: Juta & Co. Ltd.

Jacobson, H. D. (1987). *Basic Communication Skills.* London: Hodder & Stoughton.

Jones, Daniel. (1982). *Everyman's English Pronouncing Dictionary.* London: The English Language Book Society and J.M. Dent & Sons Ltd.

Jowitt, D. and Nnamomum, S. (1985). *Common Errors in English.* Essex: Longman.

Kouega, J.P. (2007). *A Dictionary of Cameroon English Usage.* Bern: Peter Lang.

Lenox-Short, A. (1970). *Effective Expression: A Course in Communication.* London: Evans Brothers Limited.

Maciver, Augus. (1981). *The New First Aid in English.* Glasgow: Robert Gibson Publisher.

Marckwardt, A. L. and Quirk, R. (1964). *A Common Language: British and American English.* London: Cox and Wyman Ltd.

McPhedran, Isabel. (1972). *Communicating in English.* London: University of London Press.

OUP. (1998). *The Concise Dictionary of Proverbs.* Oxford: Oxford University Press.

Phythian, B. A. (1980). *English Grammar.* London: Hodder & Stoughton.

_____ (1985). *Correct English.* London: Hodder & Stoughton.

Pienaar, Cathy. (1994). *Understanding Tenses: An Aid for Second Language Students.* Pretoria: Acacia Books.

Pryse, B. E. (1966). *English Without Tears.* London: Collins Clear-Type Press.

Quinn, Arthur. (1982). *Figures of Speech: 60 Ways to turn a phrase.* Layton: Gibbs.

Quirk, R. and Greenbaum. (1973). *A University Grammar of English.* Harlow, Essex: Longman.

Quirk, Randolph. (1974). *The Linguist and the English Language.* London: Edward Arnold (Publishers) Ltd.

Robinson, W. P. (1974). *Language and Social Behaviour.* Middlesex: Penguin Books.

Shaw, Harry. (1994). *Dictionary of Problem Words and Expressions*. New York: McGraw-Hill Book Company.
Temple, Michael. (1980). *A Pocket Guide to Written English*. London: John Murray Publishers.
Wood. T. F. (1979). *English Verbal Idioms*. London: Macmillan Press Ltd.
_____ (1980). *Dictionary of Colloquial Idioms*. London: Macmillan Press Ltd.
Wordall, A. J. (1975). *English Idioms for Foreign Students*. London: Longman.

Index

A
Abortion 9, 12
Accusative case 171, 204
Achu 187
Adjective 16, 17, 19, 38, 43, 44, 46, 61, 65, 66, 67, 70, 154, 156, 194, 230, 263
Adverb 1, 28, 93, 156, 164, 165, 193, 263
Advice 5
Afrikaans 83
Agnostic 15, 16
AIDS 8
Amba 187
Ambazonia 187
Ambiguity 1, 2, 3, 45, 96, 109, 128
America 67
Americanism 100, 101, 118
Antecedent 41
Article 5, 6, 7, 8, 9, 10, 28, 31, 165, 260
Asmal 15, 16
Auxiliary 168, 176, 210, 249, 250, 251

B
Bami 188
Barbarism 11, 12, 16
Barber 62
Bendskin 188
Bikini 21
Bill 73
Boyses 188
Bushfaller 189
Buy-sellam 189

C
Cabinet 12
Cameroonism 187
Camerounisme 187
Camer 189
Cameroon Pidgin English 187
Camfranglais 187
Canada 88
Capital letter 17, 19, 20, 21, 183, 185, 209, 210
Case 145, 146
Chaka 17
Chemist 2
Chess 95
Chromatics 214
Circumlocution 19, 21
Clause 98, 121, 125, 165, 172, 174, 175, 231, 240, 241, 254

Cliché 28, 35, 36
Coetzee 48
Collocation   31, 36, 38
Colloquialism   35, 36, 189
Comparative 40, 41, 42, 44, 45, 194, 222, 230
Concord 39, 40, 45, 46, 49, 50, 51, 53, 200, 211, 236, 240
Crisis 2

D
Debate 118
Defense 88
Determiner 47, 54, 55
Deuxième bureau, 190
Direct speech 142, 167, 168, 170, 199, 200, 202
Don 70
Drug 9
Dubois 49

E
Easter 69
Education 6
Eleventh province 190
English 23, 83, 1124
Environment 32
Error 75

F
Farm 15
Figurative expression   80
Fowler 149
Fun 77
Fund 77

G
Gala 47
Gear 59
Gerund 51, 52, 58, 59, 60, 65, 66, 68, 86, 87, 88
Ghana 95
Gombo 191
Graffi 191
Grammar143
    Grammarian 1

H
HIV 7
Homonym   258
Homophone 61, 62, 63, 67, 68, 70, 74, 76, 78, 79
Homophony 56, 57, 62, 67
Howler   107

I
Idiom 69, 80, 85, 210

Idiomatic expression   80, 82, 84, 150, 161, 235
Illiteracy   13, 15, 16, 17
Indirect speech   166, 169, 200, 202
Infinitive 27, 65, 66, 68, 74, 84, 86, 87, 88, 89, 91, 93, 94, 112
Initial(s)   183
Intensifier   23
Interrogative 142
Item 192

J
Jargon 213
Jiff 64
Jobajo 192
Judas 64
Juju 192

K
Kamer 192
Ke bona boloi 154
Khosi 207
Khumalo 43, 205
Kongossa 192
Kwaito 157
Kruger National Park 45, 209

L
Language 75
Letter 15, 16
Lexis   82, 96, 100
Life 82
Liquor 33
London 29
Luggage 104, 184
Luxury 62, 94

M
Mabasa 3
Machinery 40
Maize 74
Malaprop 77, 78
Malapropism 58, 77, 89, 105, 108, 261
Mashilo 23
Matango 193
Mbeki 3, 114
Misspelling   87, 99, 100, 116, 117
Modal 245
Modifier 2, 91, 93, 95, 104, 123, 124, 125, 127
Moria 15

N
Nairobi 110

Negation 97, 98, 112
Nkosi 129
Nominative case 145, 171, 172, 175, 204, 205
Noun 16, 42, 51, 53, 54, 109, 112, 126, 135, 140, 142, 146, 150, 153,
154, 170, 183, 188, 195, 229
Number 101, 116, 118, 119, 121, 123, 134, 136, 139, 140, 142,
144,
145, 164, 165, 174, 260
Numeral 119
Nyongo 193

O

Oat 42
Object 9, 148, 172, 173, 188
Objective case 171, 175, 204, 205, 226
Octopus 78
Omission 109, 127, 148
Opep 194
Orator 19
Oupa 19
Over sabi 194

P

Parenthesis 177, 179, 180
Particle 1, 2, 65, 81, 109, 112, 115, 123, 153, 162, 165, 194, 211,
233, 234
Past continuous 167
Poll 55
Pneumonia 27
Possessive 66, 205
Preposition 39, 40, 41, 117, 122, 136, 137, 138, 141, 144, 150, 159,
160,
162, 163, 165, 166, 167, 168, 169, 206, 222, 230, 254, 255
Present 166
Pretoria 106
Principle 78
Pronoun 53, 65, 123, 126, 145, 146, 147, 149, 150, 151, 153, 154,
170, 171, 172, 173, 174, 175, 179, 181, 205
Pronunciation 13
Punctuation 131, 155, 183, 185
Python 3

Q

Qualifier 153, 159, 160

Quantifier 135, 136, 188, 189, 190, 192

Queen 21

Quadruped 78

Quotation marks 183

R

Redundancy 22 ,222, 225, 226

Relative pronoun 125, 128

Reported speech 143, 166, 167, 168, 169, 199, 200, 201, 202

Roger Miller 115

S

Saka 195

Sawa 195

Scientist 8

Sekepe 8

Sex 47

Sipho 24

Slang 36

Soccer 43

Soya 195

Speech 141, 142

Stimulus 108

Subject 29, 42, 53, 54, 111, 173, 236

Subjective case 171, 204

Subjunctive mood 149, 175, 209, 210, 211, 212

Sunbath 52

Sunny Park 44

Superlative 36, 43, 45, 180

Synonym 78, 152

T

Tautology 157, 161, 183, 184, 221, 222, 223, 225, 227, 231, 233

Tense 163, 191, 193, 199, 200, 209, 211, 212, 232, 236, 238, 239,
240, 241, 242, 247, 248, 249, 254, 255, 262

Takumbeng 196

Tchamassi 196

Tobassi 196

Turf 108

U

UNESCO 8

UNISA 21

Union Buildings 131

V

Verb 49, 50, 51, 55, 57, 58, 61, 65, 71, 86, 89, 93, 111, 114,

115, 136, 137, 139, 144, 161,
172, 173, 174, 188, 189, 198,
200,
203,
209, 210, 231, 232, 233, 235,
241, 245, 247, 248, 252, 253, 262
Verbosity 26, 122, 168
Virus 7
Vocalnologist 19
Voom 196
Voum 196
Vowel 5

W
Waa 197
Wandaa 197
Wata 197
Wata fufu 197
White stuff 197
Wolowoss 197

Z
Zama-Zama 102
Zulu 17, 98

www.ingramcontent.com/pod-product-compliance
Lightning Source LLC
Chambersburg PA
CBHW051218300426
44116CB00006B/622